Thinking Globally About World Politics:
Beyond Global IR

Pinar Bilgin · Karen Smith

Thinking Globally About World Politics: Beyond Global IR

palgrave
macmillan

Pinar Bilgin
Bilkent University
Ankara, Türkiye

Karen Smith
Leiden University
Leiden, The Netherlands

Stellenbosch University
Stellenbosch, South Africa

ISBN 978-3-031-56571-7   ISBN 978-3-031-56572-4   (eBook)
https://doi.org/10.1007/978-3-031-56572-4

Cover illustration: © John Rawsterne/patternhead.com

This Palgrave Macmillan imprint is published by the registered company Springer Nature Switzerland AG
The registered company address is: Gewerbestrasse 11, 6330 Cham, Switzerland

If disposing of this product, please recycle the paper.

PREFACE

Thinking Globally About World Politics: Beyond Global IR embraces thirty plus years of effort into addressing IR's Eurocentric limitations. The so-called globalising turn is much more recent and is informed by the former, but not always explicitly so. In our understanding, thinking globally involves curiosity about what others think about the world, making a sustained effort to locate the knowledge they have produced, and recognise our/their past and present contributions to what we otherwise view as 'European' ideas, practices, and institutions. Accordingly, we envision thinking globally about world politics as an approach that would orientate students of world politics to consider the world by appreciating others (whoever or wherever they may be) not as mere objects of world politics but as fellow (read: coeval) knowledge producers; by reflecting on our/their geocultural context while remaining cognisant of how those contexts have been worlded by IR (the discipline) and ir (world politics). The 'beyond' is about moving forward first by looking back and worlding aforementioned efforts into addressing IR's Eurocentric limitations (Chapter 2 and Postscript), next by taking stock of the approaches that are currently available (Chapter 3), and finally by exploring what 'thinking globally' means in practice through focusing on the study of (international) security and foreign policy (Chapters 4 and 5).

What we label as 'thinking globally about world politics' is offered not as an alternative to but as a critical engagement with IR. Alternatives to IR have been proposed by others and we engage with them, but our aim is not that. Accordingly, we will sidestep the debates on the state of the discipline and instead explore different ways in which students of world politics could begin to think globally and design their own research projects.

We envision two main audiences for this book: students and fellow scholars. The book addresses its readers as researchers who seek to go beyond their existing training and learn about (if not move toward) thinking globally about world politics. This book would be of particular relevance to postgraduate courses that engage with the question of how to do IR in a more inclusive, globalised way (these are becoming increasingly popular, largely as a result of student demand). In addition, it would be of interest to more general IR (theory) and Research Methods courses.

Our approach is informed by our own life experience in the Global South. Pinar Bilgin began her studies in Turkey receiving a BA and MA from two different universities. After receiving an MSc and PhD in Aberystwyth, she returned to Ankara, where she has worked since 2000. Karen Smith received her BA, MA and PhD in South Africa, where she worked until 2017, before moving to the Netherlands. We have both been involved in initiatives aimed at addressing IR's Eurocentric limitations since the early 2000s, researching, publishing, and teaching with a view to furthering this effort. Both of us were a part of the 'geocultural epistemologies' project organised by Arlene Tickner and Ole Waever in the mid-2000s. Pinar was co-programme chair (with Lily Ling) of the 2015 ISA conference under Amitav Acharya's presidency, which put 'Global IR' on the agenda of many who were not previously aware of the above-mentioned efforts.

Ankara, Türkiye   Pinar Bilgin
Leiden, The Netherlands   Karen Smith

ACKNOWLEDGEMENTS

Pinar Bilgin would like to thank the Turkish Academy of Sciences for research support, the University of St Andrews for a month-long Global Fellowship in 2022, and Käte Hamburger Kolleg/Centre for Global Cooperation Research, University of Duisburg-Essen for a one-year-long Senior Fellowship in 2023. She would also like to acknowledge the feedback she received when she presented Chapter 4 at an MSc in International Security Studies Masterclass at St Andrews University (with special thanks to Faye Donnely for extensive feedback) and a Research Colloquium at Tübingen University (thanks to Thomas Diez). Finally, she would like to express her gratitude for conversations with Karen Smith, Vivienne Jabri, Siba Grovogui, Karin Fierke, David Blaney, and Kosuke Shimizu on the themes explored in this book.

Karen Smith would like to extend her gratitude to the many colleagues, friends, and students with whom she has had conversations over the past twenty years about various aspects of Eurocentrism in IR, and especially to Pinar for constantly challenging me to think in different ways.

We would like to thank our discussants at a special book workshop: Mine Nur Küçük, Neslihan Dikmen Alsancak, Burcu Türkoğlu Payne and Çağla Naz Aydoğan; our discussants at EISA Athens for their generous feedback: Zeynep Gülşah Çapan and Benjamin Herborth. Gülşah in particular has come to our rescue on more than one occasion. Finally, we would also like to pay tribute to Lily Ling, whose presence lives on through her work and inspiration.

CONTENTS

CHAPTER 1

Introduction

Pinar Bilgin and Karen Smith

Abstract This chapter lays out how this book draws on the scholarship of postcolonial, feminist and decolonising critics and insists that we, as students of International Relations (IR), learn from the wealth of knowledge already available when addressing the Eurocentric limitations of our/their concepts and theories. The chapter also outlines the scholarly context which the so-called globalising turn in IR is responding to, and locates itself in the broader effort to address Eurocentrism in the study of world politics. The chapter ends by laying out the structure of the book.

Keywords Eurocentrism · Contrapuntal reading · Decolonising · Global IR · Globalising turn

THE AIM

Notwithstanding the availability of a wealth of information regarding centuries of mutual learning between the world's peoples across space and time, conventional International Relations (IR) narratives understand and

P. Bilgin and K. Smith, *Thinking Globally About World Politics: Beyond Global IR*, https://doi.org/10.1007/978-3-031-56572-4_1

1

portray 'Europe'[1] as having developed autonomously, and everyone else as playing catch up. Different from conventional IR narratives, some critical IR scholarship treats the rest of the world as a source of inspiration by virtue of its cultural and temporal 'difference'.[2] What is common to both conventional and some critical IR is a failure to acknowledge centuries of co-constitutive dynamics between 'Europe' and the rest of the world. When it is acknowledged, such acknowledgment remains sporadic. Even when it is not sporadic, it remains focused on (neo-)colonial usurpation of material resources and self/other relations, while overlooking learning. Furthermore, none of it is brought to bear on IR concepts and theories. Consider how quickly the 'Global IR and Regional Worlds' agenda of ISA 2015[3] has bifurcated into critiques of globality in IR theorising on the one hand, and exploration of regions on the other, with next to no conversation in between.[4]

In this book, we follow the critiques advanced by postcolonial, feminist and decolonising approaches (Grovogui, 2006; Ling, 2002; Shilliam, 2021) and insist that we, as students of IR, learn from the wealth of knowledge already available when addressing the Eurocentric limitations of our/their concepts and theories. As opposed to, that is, asking whether theories travel as if they originate in one place alone, or inquiring into what 'others' think (whoever they may be, depending on the spatiotemporal context) as if no mutual learning took place across space and time. The implications are enormous. Conventional historical narratives have thus far informed conventional and critical IR concepts and theories through which we understand the world. Theorising from revisionist

---

[1] In our use, 'Europe' refers to the birthplace of Eurocentrism, and includes both North America and Western Europe. Although we understand the temptation to replace Eurocentrism with Western-centrism in an attempt to emphasise the role played by the United States, we think such a concern is misplaced. This is because Eurocentrism is not isolated to 'Europe'; see Çapan (2016). See below for further discussion on Eurocentrism.

[2] Consider, for example, Vivienne Jabri's (2007) critique of Foucault's initial embrace of the promises of the 1979 revolution in Iran. For an early critique of critical IR on this very point, see Krishna (1993). Also see, Agathangelou and Ling (1997), Grovogui (2006), Sajed (2012).

[3] https://www.isanet.org/Conferences/New-Orleans-2015.

[4] The emerging parallel is striking: on the one hand is the IR/Area Studies hierarchical division of labour in terms of theorising versus data supply, which has been with us for a long time. On the other hand is a new but also hierarchical division of labour between theoretical critiques of globality in IR theorising and regional explorations.

historical narratives has the potential to alter our thinking about world politics, because such narratives not only challenge Eurocentric historiography but also IR concepts and theories that have been drawn from conventional historical narratives.[5] It is in this sense that the persistence of Eurocentrism is a challenge not only for the study of the rest of the world but also for 'Europe'. Indeed, Eurocentrism circumscribes our understanding of the international not only because other parts of the world are missing, but because they are incorporated in a particular way that overlooks their contributions. While some of these contributions may be known to those attuned to History, Historical Sociology or Area Studies, they rarely get to inform IR concepts and theories. This is because the challenge of Eurocentrism is understood as a problem of geography (i.e., locatedness of people and institutions in 'Europe') that can be addressed through bringing in what is assumed to be 'absent', as opposed to reflecting on, critiquing and rethinking the very concepts and theories that have limited our understanding of the world in general—including assumptions of 'absence'.

In an attempt to address the limitations of conventional and critical IR identified above, the question at the heart of this book is *how to think globally about world politics*. In our understanding, thinking globally involves curiosity about what others think about the world, making a sustained effort to locate their knowledge, and recognise our/their past and present contributions to what we otherwise view as 'European' ideas, practices, and institutions.

THE CONTEXT

Over the years, IR has become increasingly global in terms of its reach. Yet when it comes to substance, it is not global enough. What, then, is missing? This question does not have a straightforward answer. IR is global insofar as IR teaching and research spans the globe. We learn from surveys of the field that the study of world politics is organised under Political Science or in separate IR departments around the globe (Dyer & Mangasarian, 1989; Groom & Light, 1994; Tickner & Waever, 2009). These departments are sometimes explicitly modelled after their North American counterparts, and students are trained by often using

---

[5] Examples of historically informed critical IR narratives include: Halperin (1997), Çapan (2016).

the same English-language textbooks or their translated versions (but see, Tickner & Smith, 2020). Annual meetings of the International Studies Association, which is based in the United States, regularly attract more than 5000 researchers from around the globe. Regional IR conferences convene in multiple locations beyond North America. There is also the World International Studies Committee, which is an umbrella organisation that brings together national and regional IR associations every three years, allowing scholars an opportunity to observe how IR is 'done' in other parts of the world. IR is undoubtedly global in terms of both reach and recognition.

But then, as we have become (physical or virtual) globetrotters in our professional lives, we seldom pause and ponder what it means to think globally about world politics. Even as students of IR, whose day job is to make sense of the international, we are not accustomed to paying attention to what people in other parts of the world think about the world. We lack "global literacy", to adopt Gayatri Chakravorty Spivak's (1992) term (also see, Muppidi, 2004). That is to say, we do not have the forethought to be curious about what others think about the world, let alone making a sustained effort to locate their thoughts (on paper or elsewhere). In that sense, Hamid Dabashi's (2015) polemical question, "can Europeans read?" was not entirely off the mark. Turning on its head the question 'can non-Europeans think?' Dabashi underscored that there is a rich body of thinking outside 'Europe', if only there was engagement with it (also see Shilliam, 2008). What we understand by 'engagement' goes beyond writing a customary footnote to Fanon, Du Bois, Spivak or Said, but to actually engage with them as coeval thinkers.[6] But then, the issue here is not only a 'European' failure to engage with 'non-Europeans' (to stay with Dabashi's choice of term). Students of IR in Africa, the Middle East, Latin America, or East Asia, also do not engage enough with the thinking and writings of their contemporaries in other parts of the world.

[6] If you recall the rush to decolonise IR syllabi during the protests that began earlier during the 2010s in the Global South but coincided with the Covid-19 pandemic in the Global North, well-meaning scholars invariably turned to Fanon, Du Bois, Spivak or Said, but not to their own contemporaries in IR who have been doing the hard work in the past thirty plus years. There is also a much longer history to decolonising the curriculum and/or the University efforts in postcolonial societies.

When designing IR course syllabi, for instance, the Global South[7] engages almost exclusively with the Global North (Andrews, 2022).

Given our track record in failing to engage with the thinking and writings of our coevals in other parts of the world, is there much reason to be optimistic about the current trajectory of the so-called 'globalising turn'?[8] Merely invoking the global does not miraculously globalise IR (Çapan, 2022). While IR might be global in terms of reach and recognition, we have not yet figured out how to think globally about world politics.

What is more, this is no mere academic matter. There is an urgency to learning how to think globally. Not least because of the need to come to terms with an increasingly globalising world and to embrace a plurality of ways of understanding it while at the same time remaining cognisant of how we are all facing the same planetary challenges (such as the climate crisis), albeit in different ways. Incidentally, two key contributors to the development of Postcolonial Studies, Said and Spivak, offered some of their key contributions out of a similar sense of urgency. In offering 'contrapuntal reading' in his seminal 1993 study, *Culture and Imperialism*, Said encouraged his readers to study how things are connected. At a time when students of Postcolonial Studies were following his and other scholars' lead to focus on how things are different, Said underscored that while we are different, we are also connected, and that studying the ways in which we are connected is no mere academic preoccupation. "Survival in fact is about the connections between things", Said (1993: 336) wrote.

Spivak, in turn, offered the notion of 'global literacy' to prepare her students for the realities of a world where we regularly encounter those

---

[7] We understand 'Global South' not as a geographical marker, but a notion that captures the so-called "new geography of production" (Prashad, 2013), indicating the presence of a First World in the Third World and a Third World in the First World (cf. Dados & Connell, 2012). First, Second and Third World are terms that were initially offered in 1952 to indicate the potential of the formerly colonised by drawing a parallel with the Third Estate before the French Revolution (Halperin, 1997: 1 f.1). The term Third World also has been used with a negative connotation, implying spatio-temporal difference from the First World. The term Second World is no longer used to refer to the Soviet or Eastern Bloc countries. However, concerns regarding the state of IR in Central and Eastern Europe (Drulák, 2009) suggest that the heritage of the Second World remains.

[8] We use 'globalising turn' to refer to the effort spearheaded by Amitav Acharya since 2014. The body of scholarship seeking to address IR's Eurocentric limitations has a much longer history and has informed the 'globalising turn', although such indebtedness often goes unacknowledged if not unknown.

who hail from different geocultural contexts. In Spivak's (1992: 7) formulation, becoming globally literate is about learning to "*recognize* agency in others, not simply to comprehend otherness [original emphasis]". Accordingly, becoming globally literate "allows us to sense that the other is not just a voice, but that others produce articulated texts, even as they, like us, are written in and by a text not of our own making" (Spivak, 1992: 16). As such, Spivak cautioned her readers not to reduce others to their geocultural contexts; to recognise their agency in making their world and also reflecting on it by producing their 'articulated texts', while also remaining cognisant of the eventuality that they are responding to a world that is not entirely of their own making.

In his book *The Politics of the Global*, Himadeep Muppidi drew on Spivak's idea for the study of world politics. Muppidi noted that what students of IR lack is not knowledge per se, but "knowing how to read that knowledge, knowing how to go beyond the self in understanding the world" (Muppidi, 2004: 3). This was also Spivak's emphasis as regards her own discipline of Literary Theory. Neither Spivak nor Muppidi recommended a new method for data excavation. Rather, they highlighted the need to "read the global" by raising our own awareness of knowledge that already exists.[9] Considered in light of Dabashi's polemical question highlighted above ('can Europeans read?'), thinking globally about world politics also entails *reading* globally–in other words, not only to gather empirical data, or cultivate area-specific perspectives, but by treating those who hail from and/or reside outside 'Europe' as coeval thinkers. But then, while 'thinking globally' involves 'reading globally', the former cannot be reduced to the latter. As will be discussed later in the book, a preliminary step here is to learn to be puzzled.

Accordingly, we envision thinking globally about world politics as an approach that would orientate students of world politics to consider the world by appreciating others not as mere objects of world politics but as coeval knowledge producers; by reflecting on their geocultural contexts while remaining cognisant of how those contexts have been worlded by IR (the discipline) and ir (world politics).[10] It is in line with our approach

[9] Said offered a new method, which entails reading existing texts contrapuntally. See Chapter 3.

[10] Throughout the book, we use ir as a shorthand for world politics, while remaining sensitive to the distinctions some scholars make between the study of world politics versus international relations.

of thinking globally that we acknowledge and learn from thirty plus years of effort toward addressing the Eurocentric limitations of IR. Although Amitav Acharya (2014) coined 'Global IR and Regional Worlds' in his presidential address to the International Studies Association, the beginnings of the effort toward countering the Eurocentric limitations of IR can be traced back to the mid-1980s when critical approaches were making headway into addressing IR's limitations.[11] We think it is important not to reinvent the wheel and to take stock of the tremendous work that has been done by feminist, postcolonial and decolonial scholarship.[12]

It is equally important to note that the efforts of the 1990s and early 2000s had emerged from a frustration with conventional IR's inability to make sense of the situation on the ground in parts of the Global South, and therefore had a very practical impetus. In contrast, much of the more recent scholarship on whether or not to embrace the so-called 'globalising turn' have remained either very abstract (focusing on theorising as a form of practice) or reported their own regional perspectives. The former challenges us to think in new ways about what knowledge is and how it is produced; but then, many contributions stop short of linking their insights to practices of world politics (other than theorising, that is). The latter body of work, in turn, has reported on their part of the world, often without seeking to bring their conceptions of the international to bear on prevailing (conventional or critical) IR concepts and theories. Indeed, the burgeoning literature on the globalising turn can be said to have fallen into the trap of navel gazing.

As highlighted above and will be further discussed below, part of the problem is a failure to recognise others' knowledge as 'knowledge'. But

---

[11] For a critical overview, see Bilgin (2016).

[12] A note on decolonial scholarship: In the present day, scholars who seek to decolonise IR see their task as radically different from approaches that draw from Postcolonial Studies. In particular, the former see the latter lacking in terms of 'delinking' (Mignolo, 2007) and focusing on 'action' (Chen, 2010; Tsang, 2021). That said, when we consider the thirty plus years of scholarship that sought to address IR's limitations, it is no easy feat attempting to draw a clear blue line between approaches that draw from decolonial versus postcolonial contributions (for a discussion, see Seth [2013], Bhambra [2014]). Let us also note that there is some confusion in IR literature surrounding the terms decoloniality and decolonising (the latter being the broader effort). Correspondingly, while we see our own approach to thinking globally about world politics as a critical engagement with IR, we remain sensitive to the anti-disciplinary disposition of Robbie Shilliam's *Decolonising Politics* (2021).

again, that is only part of the problem. Another part is that such knowledge, even when it is recognised as such, is relegated to exotic enclaves of the discipline—as opposed to being utilised to address the limitations of prevailing IR concepts and theories, that is. While we empathise with critical IR scholars who turn their gaze toward 'non-Europe' as a source of inspiration by virtue of its cultural and temporal 'difference', we think this should not come at the cost of leaving untouched IR as we know it.

EUROCENTRISM AS A CHALLENGE

Eurocentrism is a notion initially put forward by Samir Amin (1989) in critique of a culturalist understanding of how the world works, and the central place accorded to 'Europe' in it. The 'Europe' of Eurocentrism is not a location on a physical map but a mental map, and includes Western Europe and North America. The former is viewed as the birthplace of Eurocentrism, and the latter as having inherited it through migratory waves.

Three forms of Eurocentrism circulate in the study of world politics. Normative Eurocentrism puts 'Europe' and its interests at the centre of the research on world politics. For instance, International Security Studies has been Eurocentric from its foundation, treating stability in East-West relations and peace in the North Atlantic area as being of utmost importance for international security (Barkawi & Laffey, 2006). The very term 'Cold War' used in reference to the 1945–1989 period is Eurocentric insofar as there was nothing 'cold' about the experiences of, say, the Koreans, Vietnamese, Egyptians, Palestinians....This is the more easily recognisable form of Eurocentrism.

The second form is analytical. In this form of Eurocentrism, scholars design research by putting 'Europe' at the centre of their analytical framework. For instance, World Systems Theory has been critiqued for its Eurocentrism by virtue of treating 'Europe' not as just another region in the system, but as the originator of the world system itself (Boatcă, 2015). That 'Europe' is categorised as a continent without questioning, when it could equally be viewed as an extension of Asia, is also an instance of analytical Eurocentrism (Lewis & Wigen, 1997).

The third form is epistemological. In this form, Eurocentrism shapes the study of world politics by incorporating 'non-Europe' into prevailing IR narratives in a particular way that overlooks the role the latter has played in the making of the world as we know it. Sovereignty, state-hood and security are all conceptualised by drawing on this particular narrative, which is not only historically less-than-accurate but also conceptually deceiving. While other narratives are available, they are not treated as 'knowledge' and therefore not drawn upon when theorising about world politics. This is because, following Achille Mbembe, epistemological Eurocentrism "attributes truth only to the Western way of knowledge production" and "disregards other epistemic traditions". 'Europe' alone is accepted as capable of producing 'knowledge', while the rest of the world is portrayed as a place of "parochial wisdom, of antiquarian traditions, of exotic ways and means. Above all, of unprocessed data" (Mbembe, 2015). Insofar as IR concepts and theories, through which we make sense of the world, draw on a particular narrative about "what is said to have happened" in 'Europe' (Grovogui, 2006: 1) while failing to recognise the rest as 'knowledge', epistemological Eurocentrism fails the study of world politics here, there, and everywhere.[13] For instance, by failing to account for the colonial relationship between Belgium and the (Democratic Republic of) Congo (DRC), our notion of state (as well as sovereignty and security) is rendered limited in that we fail to capture what has allowed the DRC to 'fail' and Belgium to 'succeed'. For neither of the two states can be understood outside of their relational history, which is nowhere to be found in conventional historical narratives, but available elsewhere, in narratives that are not always recognised as 'knowledge' (Muppidi, 2004: 1–3). The failures involved are threefold: the DRC as a state failing to provide for its citizens, IR's understanding of the state as a concept failing to help its students make sense of forms of state around the world, and IR's *understanding* of Belgium and Congo as states.

None of these three forms of Eurocentrism is reducible to the post-code of scholars or institutions. While Eurocentrism has shaped the study of world politics outside of 'Europe', some of the most trenchant critiques of Eurocentrism have emerged from within North America and Western Europe. Furthermore, Western Europe's portrayal of Central and Eastern Europe has also been Eurocentric. That it is Western (but not Central and Eastern) Europe that has been the carrier of Eurocentrism has to do

---

[13] Needless to say, such limitations are not isolated to states with a past colonial relationship. Consider, for example, Halperin's (1997) analysis of capitalist development in 'Europe'.

with the uniqueness attributed to it as the purported home of the Renaissance, Reform, modernity and capitalism. But then, scholarship produced in Central and Eastern Europe is not always non-Eurocentric in its anti-Eurocentrism. Indeed, one of the most contentious issues surrounding Eurocentrism in the study of world politics pertains to how to overcome it, while avoiding 'anti-Eurocentric Eurocentrism' (Wallerstein, 1997).

As Branwen Grufydd-Jones (2006: 8) noted, "a superficial understanding of the problem of Eurocentrism would suggest that what is required is filling in the gaps, restoring the excluded narratives from beyond the confines of Europe". While this is one aspect of addressing Eurocentrism, another is addressing conventional historical narratives, which necessitates a retelling via revisionist histories. This involves recognising the role of race and empire in the making of 'Europe', as well as the constitutive role of the rest of the world in what is portrayed as 'European' ideas, practices and institutions. It also involves paying attention to events, processes and scholarship from outside 'Europe' (Jones, 2006: 12; also see, Shilliam, 2011) while at the same time remaining cognisant of 'the problem of postcolonial archives' (El-Malik & Kamola, 2017).[14] What comes next is addressing the Eurocentric limitations of our IR concepts and theories in light of these revisionist narratives. If not, conventional and critical IR concepts and theories remain untouched, which would mean reliving the fate of Area Studies scholars in that the wealth of information they have collected has rarely been brought to bear on IR theorising.

There is little room here for patting ourselves on the back for having arrived at a stage of maturity where we recognise Eurocentrism in epistemological terms. For, more often than not, students of IR continue to view the Eurocentric limitations of their field to be relevant only for studying the world outside 'Europe'. Accordingly, they worry about the limits of IR concepts and theories when they travel elsewhere in the world. For instance, Edward Said's (1978) insights in his classic *Orientalism* are understood as relevant for the study of the orientalised, often without considering the limitations of Occidentalism for our understanding of 'Europe'. However, as Fernando Coronil (1996) maintained, the former is not possible without the latter; both limit our understanding of how

---

[14] Understood as the dearth of information about the postcolonial either because of the absence of archives due to loss, elimination, or destruction, or simply because what is available is not recognised as 'archival material'. See also, Çapan (forthcoming).

the world works. Indeed, when we fail to capture how sovereignty in Western Europe, or the security community in the North Atlantic area, have evolved in constitutive relations with the rest of the world, our understanding of 'Europe' also suffers. It is in this sense that addressing Eurocentrism in IR is a problem for the study of 'Europe' as well. This is not only because we think the rest of the world's present may become the future of 'Europe' and that the latter may need to learn from the former (as in Kerner, 2018), but also because when our concepts and theories fail, they fail us all–here, there, and everywhere.

THE STRUCTURE

The emphasis of this book is not why or whether, but *how* to think globally about world politics. As Julian Saurin (2006) noted, "method (and theory) are at least as significant–perhaps more so–to the decolonization of IR than is normative or political intent." Of course the two are not separate, as one's motivation for addressing Eurocentrism will also have an impact on how one goes about answering the 'how to' question. If, for example, we assume, as Saurin (2006: 29) did, that imperialism is the fundamental problem for the study of IR, "retelling the story of the international through the perspective of another or as experienced by a historical agent who has hitherto been silenced...remains insufficient." Instead, Saurin (2006: 37) proposed that "a decolonization of IR needs to be recast as an anti-imperialism and that the first task is to explain imperialism's production and reproduction".

Each of the chapters that follow introduces and discusses novel ways of studying world politics with a view to addressing the concerns behind the globalising turn as well as thirty plus years of effort into addressing IR's Eurocentric limitations. Chapter 2 traces the trajectory of the latter by utilising one of its own methods: worlding. Contra present-day engagements with the globalising turn, the chapter does not begin but ends with it. Chapter 3 focuses on available approaches to thinking globally about world politics, including interventions that developed over thirty plus years of addressing IR's Eurocentric limitations, as well as their reincarnation as part of the globalising turn. It is the biggest chapter in the book and is co-authored so as to be as comprehensive as possible. Chapters 4 and 5 zoom in on two main subfields of IR to further highlight different ways of thinking globally about world politics. The idea is that the two authors draw on their expertise in the study of (international) security (Pinar Bilgin) and foreign policy (Karen Smith). Chapter 4 offers a critique of conventional approaches to security, highlights how the study of security in 'Europe' too has suffered, identifies the persisting limitations of critical approaches, and explores one way of thinking globally about security, by utilising the notion of 'constitutive outside'. Chapter 5 provides an overview of existing attempts at addressing the criticism of Eurocentrism in the study of foreign policy, and the sub-field of Foreign Policy Analysis in particular. It goes on to explore the case study of South African foreign policy through a relational lens. The book ends with a Postscript that provides an overview of and conversations with some scholars who have been doing the 'globalising' work, with the aim of showing that this is not a new trend in IR, and also identifying the individuals' motivations for engaging with these issues.

A final point is that none of us, regardless of where we happen to be located geographically, is immune to the constitutive power of knowing. IR has worlded all of us, as noted above. But there is an upside to this. All of us stand to benefit from learning how to think globally about world politics, wherever we happen to hail from and/or reside.

BIBLIOGRAPHY

Acharya, A. (2014). Global International Relations (IR) and Regional Worlds. *International Studies Quarterly, 58*(4), 647–659.

Agathangelou, A. M., & Ling, L. (1997). Postcolonial Dissidence within Dissident IR: Transforming Master Narratives of Sovereignty in Greco-Turkish Cyprus. *Studies in Political Economy, 54*(1), 7–38.

Amin, S. (1989). *Eurocentrism* (R. Moore, Trans. 2009 ed.). Monthly Review Press.

Andrews, N. (2022). The Persistent Poverty of Diversity in International Relations and the Emergence of a Critical Canon. *International Studies Perspectives, 23*(4), 425–449.

Barkawi, T., & Laffey, M. (2006). The Postcolonial Moment in Security Studies. *Review of International Studies, 32*(2), 329–352.

Bhambra, G. K. (2014). Postcolonial and Decolonial Dialogues. *Postcolonial Studies, 17*(2), 115–121.

Bilgin, P. (2016). *The International in Security, Security in the International.* Routledge.

Boatcă, M. (2015). The Quasi-Europes: World Regions in Light of the Imperial Difference. In T. Reifer (Ed.), *Global Crises and the Challenges of the 21st Century* (pp. 132–153). Routledge.

Çapan, Z. G. (2016). *Re-writing International Relations: History and Theory Beyond Eurocentrism in Turkey*. Rowman and Littlefield.

Çapan, Z. G. (2022). TimeSpace of the 'International'. *Cambridge Review of International Affairs, 35*(6), 811–825.

Çapan, Z. G. (forthcoming). Archives. In B. Jahn & S. Schindler (Eds.), *Elgar Encyclopedia of International Relations*. Edward Elgar.

Chen, K.-H. (2010). *Asia as Method: Toward Deimperialization*. Duke University Press.

Coronil, F. (1996). Beyond Occidentalism: Toward Nonimperial Geohistorical Categories. *Cultural Anthropology, 11*(1), 51–87.

Dabashi, H. (2015). *Can Non-Europeans Think?* Zed Books.

Dados, N., & Connell, R. (2012). The Global South. *Contexts, 11*(1), 12–13.

Drulák, P. (Ed.) (2009). Special Forum Section: International Relations (IR) in Central and Eastern Europe. *Journal of International Relations and Development, 12*(2), 168–173.

Dyer, H. C., & Mangasarian, L. (Eds.). (1989). *The Study of International Relations: The State of the Art*. Macmillan.

El-Malik, S. S., & Kamola, I. A. (Eds.) (2017). *Politics of African Anticolonial Archive*. Rowman and Littlefield.

Groom, A. J. R., & Light, M. (Eds.). (1994). *Contemporary Onternational Relations: A Guide to Theory*. Pinter Publishers.

Grovogui, S. N. (2006). *Beyond Eurocentrism and Anarchy: Memories of International Order and Institutions*. Palgrave Macmillan.

Halperin, S. (1997). *In the Mirror of the Third World: Capitalist Development in Modern Europe*. Cornell University Press.

Jabri, V. (2007). Michel Foucault's Analytics of War: The Social, the International, and the Racial. *International Political Sociology, 1*, 67–81.

Jones, B. G. (2006). Introduction: International Relations, Eurocentrism, and Imperialism. In B. G. Jones (Ed.), *Decolonizing International Relations* (pp. 1–21). Rowman and Littlefield.

Kerner, I. (2018). Beyond Eurocentrism: Trajectories Towards a Renewed Political and Social Theory. *Philosophy and Social Criticism, 44*(5), 550–570.

Krishna, S. (1993). The Importance of Being Ironic: A Poscolonial View on Critical International Relations Theory. *Alternatives, 18*(3), 385–417.

Lewis, M. W., & Wigen, K. (1997). *The Myth of Continents: A Critique of Metageography*. University of California Press.

Ling, L. H. M. (2002). *Postcolonial International Relations: Conquest and Desire between Asia and the West*. Palgrave.

Mbembe, A. (2015). *Decolonizing Knowledge and the Question of the Archive*. https://wiser.wits.ac.za/content/achille-mbembe-decolonizing-knowledge-and-question-archive-12054

Mignolo, W. D. (2007). Delinking: The Rhetoric of Modernity, the Logic of Coloniality and the Grammar of De-coloniality. *Cultural Studies, 21*(2–3), 449–514.

Muppidi, H. (2004). *The Politics of the Global.* University of Minnesota Press.

Prashad, V. (2013). *The Poorer Nations: A Possible History of the Global South.* Verso.

Said, E. W. (1978). *Orientalism.* Penguin.

Said, E. W. (1993). *Culture and Imperialism.* Knopf.

Sajed, A. (2012). The Post Always Rings Twice? The Algerian War, Poststructuralism and the Postcolonial in IR theory. *Review of International Studies, 38*(1), 141–163.

Saurin, J. (2006). International Relations as the Imperial Illusion; or, the Need to Decolonize IR. In B. G. Jones (Ed.), *Decolonizing International Relations* (pp. 23–42). Rowman and Littlefield.

Seth, S. (2013). *Postcolonial Theory and International Relations: A Critical Introduction.* Routledge.

Shilliam, R. (2008). The Enigmatic Figure of the Non-Western Thinker in International Relations. *Antepodium.* http://www.victoria.ac.nz/atp/art icles/pdf/Shilliam-2009.pdf

Shilliam, R. (2021). *Decolonizing Politics: An Introduction.* Polity Press.

Shilliam, R. (Ed.). (2011). *International Relations and Non-Western thought: Imperialism, Colonialism, and Investigations of Global Modernity.* Routledge.

Spivak, G. C. (1992). Teaching for the Times. *The Journal of the Midwest Modern Language Association, 25*(1), 3–22.

Tickner, A. B., & Smith, K. (Eds.). (2020). *International Relations from theGlobal South: Worlds of difference.* Routledge.

Tickner, A. B., & Waever, O. (Eds.). (2009). *Global Scholarship in International Relations: Worlding Beyond the West.* Routledge.

Tsang, M. (2021). *Decolonial? Postcolonial? What Does it Mean to 'Decolonise Ourselves'?* Retrieved from https://blogs.ncl.ac.uk/decolonisesml/2021/01/ 21/decolonial-postcolonial-what-does-it-mean-to-decolonise-ourselves/

Wallerstein, I. (1997). Eurocentrism and its Avatars: The Dilemmas of Social Science. *New Left Review, 226*, 93–108.

CHAPTER 2

Toward Thinking Globally about World Politics

Pinar Bilgin

Abstract This chapter traces the trajectory of the efforts to address International Relations (IR)'s Eurocentric limitations by utilising one of its own methods: worlding. It begins by considering two different understandings of worlding and underscores the need to utilise both at the same time so that we can make sense of the apparent tension between IR being global and yet not global enough. Next, the chapter traces the trajectory of the scholarship that has sought to address IR's Eurocentric limitations by worlding this body of work in terms of both the situatedness and constitutive power of knowing. In doing so, the chapter identifies key moves, openings and closures, as scholars have reflected on US hegemony in the study of IR, responded to its persistence notwithstanding efforts to pluralise the discipline, diagnosed the cultural production of a particular way of doing IR as 'IR', inquired into IR in other parts of the world, and called for a 'Global IR and Regional Worlds'.

Keywords Worlding · Eurocentrism · Hegemony · Pluralism · Paradigm · Incommensurability · Global IR · Regional worlds

© The Author(s), under exclusive license to Springer Nature
Switzerland AG 2024
P. Bilgin and K. Smith, *Thinking Globally About World Politics: Beyond Global IR*, https://doi.org/10.1007/978-3-031-56572-4_2

INTRODUCTION

If IR is both global and not global enough, where does that leave us? To be able to reconcile these seemingly contradictory conditions, I turn to 'worlding' as an approach. In so doing, I trace the trajectory of the efforts to address IR's Eurocentric limitations by utilising one of their own approaches.

In the study of IR, 'worlding' is often employed to reflect on the geocultural situatedness of knowing. However, there is another aspect to worlding as articulated by Spivak (1985, 1999), which is about the constitutive power of knowing. While these two understandings of worlding were introduced to IR around the same time, it has been the former (worlding as [geocultural] situatedness) that has shaped contemporary debates on the limitations of IR, and not the other (worlding as constitutive).

The chapter begins by considering these two different understandings of worlding and underscoring the need to utilise both understandings at the same time so that we can make sense of IR being global and not global enough. Next, I will trace the trajectory of the scholarship that has sought to address IR's Eurocentric limitations[1] by worlding this body of work in terms of *both* the situatedness *and* constitutive power of knowing.[2] I do this by identifying key moves, openings, and closures as scholars reflected on US hegemony in the study of IR; responded to its persistence notwithstanding efforts at pluralising the discipline; diagnosed the cultural production of a particular way of doing IR as 'IR'; inquired into IR in other parts of the world, and called for a 'Global IR and Regional Worlds'.[3]

---

[1] Early scholars discussed here did not always problematise IR's limitations in terms of 'Eurocentrism'. Yet, their explorations of the parochialism of US IR and its persistence have paved the way for others' identification of Eurocentrism as key for addressing IR's continuing limitations.

[2] On both/and, see Chapter 3.

[3] Please note that unlike in Chapter 3, here I merely periodise the works I discuss. I trace the trajectory of this body of scholarship in roughly historical terms to highlight how it has worlded and been worlded by IR. I do not mean to suggest that these 'moves, openings and closures' were entirely intentional on the part of the scholars. They were consequential nevertheless.

WORLDING AND WORLDING: (GEOCULTURAL) SITUATEDNESS AND THE CONSTITUTIVE POWER OF KNOWING

It is through feminist scholarship that the notion of worlding was first introduced to IR. Jan Jindy Pettman's (1996) book *Worlding Women* argued that it was high time everyone recognised "that women are in the world and in world politics". For Pettman (1996: ii), worlding women was meant to highlight and address the gendered nature of IR so that it would be revised to include "the different worlds of those outside the powerful centres and classes...in our understanding" of world politics. Following Pettman, worlding IR was understood by scholars as opening up the study of world politics to include the thinking of those who are differently situated.

Unbeknownst to Pettman's readers in IR, Spivak had offered a more far-reaching understanding of worlding back in 1985 when she cautioned against focusing on (geocultural) situatedness alone. At the time, Spivak contextualised her discussion with reference to the temptation to become a 'native informant' speaking on behalf of the Third World (author's choice of term). It is a temptation for a scholar hailing from the Third World, she argued, insofar as one finds a ready-made role to play and language to speak. Spivak (1999: 211) thought that if scholars hailing from the Third World focused only on the production of knowledge that reflected their positionality as an 'other' to their First World colleagues, they would lose sight of the eventuality "that it was the colonisers' writings that depicted the lands that they encountered as if it was 'uninscribed earth'". Put differently, Spivak's understanding of worlding was not limited to reflecting on geocultural situatedness. She also sought to capture the constitutive power of knowledge produced by the colonisers. Here is an example of Spivak's (1999: 211) analysis of an early nineteenth century letter by an assistant to the then British governor of India:

> He [the author of the letter] is actually engaged in consolidating the Self of Europe by obliging the native to cathect the space of the Other on his home ground [...] He is worlding their own world, which is far from mere uninscribed earth anew, by obliging them to domesticate the alien as master. Much 'thicker descriptions of this, are, of course, to be found in settler colonies—a worlding visited upon 'native' Americans, Black South Africans, Australian Aborigines, the Suomis of Northern Europe...

For Spivak, worlding was meant to understand how narratives of the colonised worlded the Third World, thereby helping to shape them and those who spoke on their behalf. The scholar was interested in the ways in which the worlding of the Third World shaped peoples' understandings of themselves as 'others' to the First World 'self'. In a nutshell, Spivak explored worlding as the constitutive power of knowing *as well as* the situatedness of the authors (also see Ahluwalia and Sullivan [2001] on Said's notion of 'worlding').

Reading Spivak from today's vantage point where scholars are oftentimes reduced to their geocultural positionality, the author's caution comes across as prescient. Indeed, Spivak insisted that scholars reflect on the ways in which their geocultural situatedness is a product of previous writings through which colonised space was "brought into the 'world', that is, made to exist as part of a world essentially constructed by a Eurocentrism" (Ashcroft et al., 2009: 225). Accordingly, reflecting on our geocultural situatedness alone may result in overlooking the ways in which the colonial encounter and the body of knowledge produced in and through that encounter has worlded the world. The colonial encounter needs analysing not only in terms of the usurpation of material resources and/or self/other dynamics, but also in terms of constituting ideas regarding how the world works. Hence Spivak's (1985: 247) resolve in "documenting and theorising the itinerary of the consolidation of Europe as a sovereign subject, indeed sovereign and subject". Failing to reflect on the worlding of the Third World by the colonisers, Spivak (1985: 247) cautioned, scholars would likely end up thinking/writing about the Third World only "as distant cultures, exploited but with rich intact heritages waiting to be recovered, interpreted and curricularised in English translation".

Here is our takeaway from this discussion: we cannot presume those living in other parts of the world to have remained untouched by IR's attempts to understand and narrate the world. But then, if IR in other parts of the world comes across as similar, especially to those who understand the so-called 'globalising turn'[4] in terms of a search for 'exotic difference', such similarity need not be written off as 'unthinking emulation' but could be treated as a research puzzle into scholarly agency

---

[4] We use 'globalising turn' to refer to the effort spearheaded by Amitav Acharya since 2014. The body of scholarship seeking to address IR's Eurocentric limitations has a much longer history.

and reflexivity (Bilgin, 2008).[5] Worlding as inquiring into the constitutive power of knowing is most relevant as we explore the state of IR in general and the trajectory of efforts to address IR's limitations in particular. The idea here is not that IR scholars give up on the task of reflecting on the geocultural situatedness of knowing. Rather, our task becomes one of reflecting on the ways in which our geocultural situatedness is not independent of IR or ir.[6]

Worlding IR

As students of world politics, we are accustomed to hearing two stories about the origins of IR. One story traces it to post-World War I United Kingdom where concerns with preventing yet another devastating worldwide war resulted in the founding of what is viewed as the world's first Chair devoted to the study of world politics, in Aberystwyth. The other story traces it to post-World War II United States where concerns with making the world safe for the pursuit of US interests was followed by public and private investment into the study of IR in institutions of higher education and think tanks in the United States. Revisionist scholarship, in turn, has revealed two things: that IR was born multiple times in multiple places around the world (Thakur & Smith, 2021); and that the two conventional stories of IR have left out other contributions to international thought produced in those very settings in the UK and US—especially black and women's thought (Hutchings, 2023; Vitalis, 2018).

My goal here is not to offer another story of IR that fills in the gaps created/left by these two stories. Rather, I will focus on key moves and openings as well as closures. The idea is to trace how students of world politics gradually came to reflect on their discipline being less than global, the solutions they offered, and the challenges they encountered along the way. In so doing, I will consider *both* the geocultural situatedness of these key works, *and* the ways in which they helped constitute IR.[7]

---

[5] See the Postscript for further discussion on my own scholarly reflections.

[6] Throughout the book, we use ir as a shorthand for world politics, while remaining sensitive to the distinctions some scholars make between the study of world politics versus international relations.

[7] For a discussion on 'both/and', see Chapter 3.

Reflections on US Hegemony in the Study of World Politics

I will begin with Stanley Hoffman's (1977) article entitled "An American Social Science: International Relations", which offered an early analysis of the parochialism of IR in the US. Hoffman is frequently cited in writings that focus on the limitations of IR, especially by those who consider those limitations to be rooted in IR being 'An American Social Science'. That said, Hoffman's article is one of those works that is more frequently cited than closely read. For, contrary to what his title seems to imply (and many who cite his article seem to presume) Hoffman's (1977: 41) study is not a celebration of US IR, but rather "a set of reflections on the specific accomplishments and frustrations of a particular field of scholarship".

According to Hoffman (1977: 45), IR took the form it did due to a specific set of circumstances in post-war US, which he analysed in terms of "intellectual predispositions, political circumstances, and institutional opportunities". Insofar as these circumstances did not come together in other parts of the world, argued Hoffman, IR was and would remain an "American Social Science", serving "as a model and as lever" for others. In the quote below, Hoffman (1977: 47) explained, rather matter-of-factly, how US foreign policy shaped the study of world politics:

> Almost inevitably, a concern for America's conduct in the world blended with a study of international relations, for the whole world seemed to be the stake of the American-Soviet confrontation...To study United States foreign policy was to study the international system. To study the international system could not fail to bring one back to the role of the United States.[8]

Hoffman (1977: 59) concluded that in the future, IR would need to distance itself from the US perspective "toward that of the weak and the revolutionary". But then, how was this supposed to happen? For, when Hoffman looked around the world, he did not recognise any other IR but that of the US. He also did not see the promise of it happening anytime soon as long as the specific set of circumstances that allowed for the emergence of IR in the United States did not transpire elsewhere. Hoffman (1977: 49) wrote,

---

[8] It is important to highlight here that Hoffman did not reflect on how race and gender dynamics shaped domestic politics and foreign policy in the United States, thereby remaining oblivious to key constitutive elements of IR as an 'American social science'.

scholars will not have the motivation or receive the impulse necessary to turn individual efforts into a genuine scientific enterprise, and will either turn to other fields with more solid traditions or merely reflect, more or less slavishly, and with some delays, American fashions, or else there will be often brilliant contributions, but unconnected and unsupported: A Hedley Bull in Australia (and England), a Pierre Hassner in France, to name just these two, do not make a discipline.

Worlding Hoffman's 1977 article, two observations are in order. One, while Hoffman highlighted how IR scholars in the US mistook their foreign policy concerns for 'IR', he did not reflect on his own geocultural situatedness as a scholar. For, Hoffman already had an image of what IR was supposed to look like when he went looking for it around the world. Put differently, Hoffman offered a very parochial analysis of the parochialism of US IR. What renders parochialism a challenge is not that scholars in different parts of the world may have their narrow (geographical or topical) areas of concentration, but that they mistake their own particular window on the world for the universal (Bilgin, 2016). Hoffman viewed US IR as the only way to do 'IR' and regarded its non-appearance in other places as an 'absence'.

But then (and this is the second observation) Hoffman's article worlded IR insofar as future scholars took his conclusions as the starting point for their own reflections on the state of the discipline. If you do a quick Google Scholar search of the works that cite Hoffman's article, you will observe a steadily increasing number of citations from the late 1970s until today. This is what I mean by Hoffman's 1977 article having worlded IR—not only because of US prevalence in the study of IR, but also in the ways in which such prevalence has been made sense of. In time, IR scholars have inquired into US prevalence as such in terms of geocultural situatedness of IR in the US, but not in terms of the constitutive power of knowing. At best, such prevalence was explained away as mere emulation of the US. While mimicry cannot be overlooked, the agency of US government institutions and foundations in making it happen (Parmar, 2002) or that of local scholars (Bilgin, 2008) should not be discounted.

Key move: reflecting on geocultural situatedness of IR in the US. Opening: identifying the parochialism of US IR.

Closure: failing to reflect on the constitutive power of knowing (i.e., the entrenchment of US IR as 'IR').

Responses to the Persistence of US Hegemony in a More Plural IR Discipline

Next, I will look at two studies: Hayward Alker and Thomas Biersteker's (1984) article entitled "The Dialectics of World Order: Notes for a Future Archaeologist of International Savoir Faire", and K. J. Holsti's (1985) book *The Dividing Discipline: Hegemony and Diversity in International Theory*. These two studies took stock of how IR was taught by looking at graduate level course syllabi in the United States (Alker and Biersteker) and IR textbooks in the US, UK, France, Korea, India, Canada, Australia and Japan (Holsti). Different from Hoffman, both studies highlighted the existence of a plurality of theories in the US and around the world.

To begin with Alker and Biersteker, their study was designed to reflect on the parochialism of US IR and highlight the limitations of Hoffman's reflections. Alker and Biersteker (1984: 128) found that

> most 'leading' American instructors of courses on theories of international relations were exceedingly parochial. This was true even during the enlightened era of the early 1980s. Not only were the bulk of the readings on their syllabuses written by other American scholars, but those readings were also derived almost exclusively from...behavioural science. This means that the questions asked, the values assumed, the issues addressed, and the debates considered...have been nearly all addressed from within the narrow confines of a single epistemological tradition.

Alker and Biersteker's (1984: 137) conclusion was that IR needed "an increase in international *savoir faire*, the ability rationally and persuasively to navigate one's scientific investigations across and through a variety of paradigmatic contexts."

Different from Hoffman, Alker and Biersteker recognised the study of world politics in different parts of the world as 'IR'. They identified three approaches: traditional, radical/Marxist, and behavioural science. The authors highlighted that while behavioural science was dominant in the United States, the other two approaches were also visible; and that traditional and radical/Marxist approaches dominated in the other parts of the world. In so doing, Alker and Biersteker offered a corrective to what they regarded as Hoffman's "dismal view of international relations abroad" (Alker & Biersteker, 1984: 140 f.147) and opened up space for the study of world politics in other parts of the world as 'IR'. Holsti looked at IR textbooks in six countries so as to see which approaches prevailed and where. He observed that while Realism dominated everywhere, other theories also had a presence in other parts of the world. Reflecting on his findings, Holsti considered two issues to be problematic for the future of IR. One was what he regarded as a lack of dialogue between theories. Hence the title of his book, *The Dividing Discipline*. Another issue identified by Holsti (1985: 127) was that the perspectives of those outside North America and Western Europe did not get represented in IR textbooks, which led him to conclude that "international theory barely exists outside the anglophone countries".

Worlding these two studies in terms of their geocultural situatedness, we see that they reflect the 1980s' recognition of a plurality of IR theories in the United States and elsewhere. That said, when reporting on the predominance of Realism over other theories, Holsti read this as an almost natural development, thereby failing to reflect on the agency of the US, including scholarships, research grants, think tanks and foundations. Put differently, Holsti's lament about the persistence of US hegemony suggested that he was oblivious to the ways in which US IR worlded the world. As such, Holsti's parochialism was only one step removed from Hoffman.

While Holsti did recognise the study of world politics outside the United States as 'IR', and acknowledged a plurality of theories being taught in the United States and elsewhere, he understood the persistence of US hegemony as a consequence of what he viewed as an absence of 'IR theory' in other parts of the world. This was because Holsti carried with him a picture of what 'IR theory' is supposed to look like when he went looking for it elsewhere in the world. When he failed to find what he was looking for, Holsti did not reflect on his understanding of 'IR theory' or ask whether thinking theoretically about world politics might look different in other parts of the world.[9] In contrast to Holsti, Alker and Biersteker did locate scholars from outside 'Europe' who thought

---

[9] Writing more than two decades later, when Acharya and Buzan (2007) asked "why is there no non-Western IR theory?" (see below) they echoed Holsti's preconceived idea as to what 'IR theory' looks like (see below).

theoretically about world politics (one contemporary and others classical: Cardoso, Lenin and Mao), discussing their strengths and weaknesses.

Worlding these two works in terms of the constitutive power of knowing brings to the fore the issue of 'incommensurability', or rather, how concerns with incommensurability stalled the progress of efforts toward addressing IR's Eurocentric limitations. In *The Structure of Scientific Revolutions*, Thomas Kuhn (1962) had adopted a history of science approach and offered the notion of incommensurability to highlight how different theories cannot be evaluated in terms of another insofar as they use different concepts and measurements. That Alker and Biersteker on the one hand and Holsti on the other were concerned with incommensurability of IR theories reflected the influence of Kuhn (1962) on the social sciences at the time. However, these two studies revealed very different interpretations of the implications of Kuhnian ideas for IR. For Alker and Biersteker, incommensurability did not mean total incommunicability between theories. They thought that incommensurability left room for debates on disciplinary discussions and that IR's limitations could be addressed in a dialectical process. In contrast, while Holsti recognised a plurality of IR theories, he did not come across as pluralist. On the contrary, he lamented that a plurality of theories meant that IR would never become a 'normal science' (which he understood as populated by commensurate theories that can be evaluated through each other's categories and standards).

Concerns with incommensurability as formulated by Holsti had lasting implications for the calls to address IR's limitations.[10] In the 1980s and 1990s, such concerns were taken at face value and used as an excuse by some to close themselves off to conversations especially if they involved critique (Wight, 2012). While this 'excuse' was utilised by both conventional and critical IR scholars, the latter found themselves on the defensive more often than not.[11] As will be discussed below, by the mid-1990s, when scholars who sought to address IR's Eurocentric limitations began to find their way into the field, concerns related to incommensurability circumscribed the potential for their critique to gain any significant ground.

---

[10] This is not to imply that Alker's work was without influence on future generations; see especially Marlin-Bennett (2012). Also note that Tickner and Waever's edited volume (see below) is dedicated to Alker.

[11] See, for example, responses by critical IR scholars: Guzzini (1993), Waever (1996).

Key move: inquiring into the persistence of US hegemony in IR studies.

Opening: recognition of a plurality of theories as 'IR'.

Closure: Holsti's narrow definition of 'theory' and understanding of incommensurability as incommunicability.

Diagnoses of the Cultural Production of a Particular Way of Doing IR as 'IR'

Here, I will focus on Siba Grovogui's (1996) monograph entitled *Sovereigns, Quasi-sovereigns and Africans: Race and Self-determination in International Law*, and Stephen Chan's (1996) collection of essays entitled *Towards a Multicultural Rashomon Paradigm in International Relations*. Both studies offered ground-breaking critiques of the cultural production of a particular way of doing IR as 'IR'.

Grovogui was trained in International Law (IL) and later turned to IR, not necessarily looking for solutions but rather getting exasperated with the insights IL was able to offer about issues he was interested in. IR not only failed to offer a solution, Grovogui argued, but it was a part of the problem. In the preface to *Sovereigns, Quasi-Sovereigns and Africans*, Grovogui clarified how this was not the book he initially set out to write: "Initially, I wanted to write a strictly jurisprudential analysis of sovereignty, colonial rule, and the reestablishment of sovereignty through postcolonial self-determination in Namibia, formerly South West Africa" (Grovogui, 1996: ix). He changed his mind, Grovogui (1996: x) wrote, once he got deeper into the archives and encountered document after document that showed how the "postwar settlements, in particular the mandate system, radically rejected the humanity of Africans and other colonial peoples". Realising that these representations were no mere expediency but were "at the core of Western philosophic systems since the Middle Ages, and of international legal constructs since the Protestant Reformation" and that "there were connections between historical philosophical systems and the structures of international order" (Grovogui, 1996: x), he wrote the book under consideration. Grovogui's (1996: 4) book was designed to analyse the discourses of international law and politics, so as to be able to show how "[w]hatever the immediate objects of the norms of international politics, they have been marked by the obsession and the capacity of the West to dominate non-Europeans in a variety of hierarchical orders".

Grovogui noted that European actors' relationship with non-European others (author's choice of term) has changed throughout history and that it was only after 1492 that they acquired a new quality, resulting in the "discursive obliteration of Africans' humanity" (Grovogui, 1996: 5; cf. McGrane, 1989). In time, the discourses of international law and politics generated "[their] own economy: its generative rules, naming systems, preconditions and implications", argued Grovogui (1996: 9), whereby Africa was incorporated into the international order and placed "at the bottom of the European-inspired universe". Accordingly, Grovogui's book showed how the jurisprudential issues that he initially wanted to write about were a product of the ways in which Africa has been worlded by aforementioned writings on international law and politics. If IR was not able to offer insights into such questions, this was because IR itself was a cultural product of this particular way of looking at the world and was dedicated to solving the problems of the world as understood by one cultural group (also see, Grovogui, 2001, 2002, 2006).

While Grovogui offered a historically informed diagnosis of IR as a cultural product, Chan's collection of essays focused on twentieth century world politics. The author pointed to several episodes in world politics (including the Iranian revolution, the Qaddafi regime in Libya, and China's 'three worlds theory') to show how they could not be grasped through conventional IR concepts and theories. It was not only IR's inability to account for these instances of world politics that confounded Chan (1996: 36), but IR scholars' failure to be puzzled[12] "where neither conventional analysis nor any paradigm could fit". It was sociologists and political anthropologists who took note of these instances, observed Chan, but not IR scholars. As such, he identified IR's limitations not in terms of the absence of voices from outside North America and Western Europe (as with Hoffmann and Holsti) but in terms of IR scholars' lack of curiosity as regards those instances of world politics that could not be accounted for within our existing concepts and theories. Chan's diagnosis being: IR is a cultural product that mistook its particularity for the universal. So long as IR scholars remained oblivious to the cultural

---

[12] See Chapter 3 for a discussion on learning to be puzzled.

production of a particular way of doing IR as 'IR', concluded Chan, they would be unable to see IR's limitations, let alone begin to address them. What did Chan propose by way of addressing IR's limitations? It was already hinted at in the title of his book, which reminded his readers of Akira Kurosawa's celebrated film Rashomon.[13] The film told the story of the murder of a samurai and the raping of his wife from the perspective of several protagonists' differing perspectives, without privileging either one of their stories or questioning their truthfulness. Underscoring the multiplicity of narratives, Chan (1996: 118–119) wrote:

> Here, the same event provided different protagonistic representations of it. Each representation was made with different language (Japanese speakers will know this much more than readers of the subtitles); each reflected a different psychology and each reflected the different ontological condition of the protagonist concerned, reflecting his or her position in society, the consequences he or she faced, with each believing he or she spoke the truth. The Rashomon condition is the true condition which IR faces.

In a joint piece with Vivienne Jabri, Chan clarified implications of the Rashomon condition, noting that

> a world of inclusions must take into account that not every epistemology is like ours, and that some are very different because of very different ontologies. Communication, debate, and even explanation are possible. Concurrence of imagination and understanding are not always possible. (Jabri & Chan, 1996: 110)

In this sense, Jabri and Chan echoed Alker and Biersteker's view that incommensurability was not an obstacle to communication. But then, at the time, Holsti's understanding of incommensurability as incommunicability still prevailed in IR.

This brings us to worlding these two books in terms of the geocultural situatedness of knowing. Let me begin by noting that they were published at a time when critical IR scholars were seeking to register 'dissent' and 'celebrate difference' (George & Campbell, 1990). Indeed, beginning from the early 1980s, the field had witnessed concerted efforts toward this end. By the late 1990s, when Chan's and Grovogui's books

---

[13] https://www.imdb.com/title/tt0042876/

were published, critical IR had gained significant ground. But then, it was these very accomplishments of critical IR scholarship in opening up the discipline that rendered visible those limitations that remained, as analysed by Chan and Grovogui.

To revisit the issue of disciplinary closure highlighted above, what stifled the efforts designed to follow up on Chan and Grovogui's critique was a disciplining move on the part of IR scholars who played the incommensurability card. Here is Chan's (1996: 72) reflection on the pushback he received:

> In international relations, the movement towards multiple theories of a few things can only enrich debate, but the fear may be that it will disorder debate when, hitherto, the entire professional thrust has been to order it. In applying order of a particular sort, it might be said that there have not been three paradigms but a single western paradigm.

Writing ten years later after the publication of the study under consideration, Grovogui (2006, 20–21) reflected on the ways in which "the discipline endorses the exclusivity and sufficiency of certain modes only at the expense of the pursuit and breadth of knowledge...which might stretch and challenge them in multiple ways".

That said, during the 1990s and early 2000s, Chan's arguments did resonate with a handful of scholars including Roland Bleiker (1997) who grew impatient with disciplinary debates, suggesting that we "Forget IR Theory", as well as Chan's close collaborators who edited *The Zen of International Relations: IR Theory From East to West* (2001) and a special issue of the journal *Global Society* (2003) entitled "Locating the 'I' in 'IR': Dislocating Euro-American Theories". Viewed from today's vantage point, where scholars invite fellow students of IR to consider multiple worlds (Ling, 2002) and a pluriverse (Blaney & Tickner, 2017; Trownsell et al., 2022), Chan's advocacy, during the 1990s of embracing 'the Rashomon condition of IR' and considering ontology over epistemology (Jabri & Chan, 1996) comes across as prescient. But then, the gradual way this body of scholarship had made its mark seems to have less to do with the substance of what was on offer and more to do with the field's receptiveness to what they had on offer. For, while critical IR 'celebrated difference' and made room for scholarship introducing other ways of knowing the world, the way this was done, that is, by "[consigning] non-Western thought to the realm of sheer curiosity, to be interrogated by modernity but not allowed to interrogate modernity" (Pasha 2011: 219) circumscribed the room for scholarly exchange, let alone for explorations of multiple beginnings of modernity (see, esp. Bhambra, 2007).

At this moment in time, where IR's pattern of 'unseeing' of scholarship by those identified as 'different' (by virtue of their gender, race, culture and/or religion or their intersections) is being revealed and discussed in rich studies (Hutchings, 2023; Inayatullah & Blaney, 2004; Pasha, 2017; Vitalis, 2018), some are likely to suspect that 'difference' alone explains their contemporaries' failure to engage with Chan and Grovogui.[14] Another possible explanation could be found in the fact that both Chan and Grovogui's early works looked at African thought and/or cases as illustrations, thereby making it easier to designate their contributions as Area Studies—acknowledged but not allowed to interrogate disciplinary IR (Chan 1985; Grovogui 1996).

Be that as it may, there is also the issue of 'un/timeliness' to be considered. Their peers seem to have "underestimate[d] the novelty and originality of...[Chan and Grovogui's] insights at the time of writing" to paraphrase Stuart Hall (2021: 342).[15] Indeed, when introducing a forum on Grovogui's (2006) book *Beyond Eurocentrism and Anarchy: Memories of International Order and Institutions* ten years after its publication, Mahmood Mamdani et al. 2016: 174) made the observation that it "was a little ahead of its time". But then, what is un/timeliness if not the receptiveness of one's contemporaries to the ideas one offers?

The issue of 'un/timeliness' bring us back to worlding in terms of the constitutive power of knowing. Judging by Google Scholar citation figures alone, Chan and Grovogui did not seem to have been engaged by their contemporaries. That said, Postcolonial IR started to take shape during the 1990s, beginning to make its mark in the writings of a small circle of scholars (see, for example: Agathangelou & Ling, 1997; Blaney & Inayatullah, 1994; Darby & Paolini, 1994; Inayatullah & Blaney, 1996; Krishna, 1993, 1999; Ling, 1996; Muppidi, 1999; Slater, 1998). While this body of work has informed the 'globalising turn' (see below), such indebtedness often goes unknown and unacknowledged.

---

[14] See, Chan (2022) and Grovogui (2013). On biographies, see the Postscript.

[15] See, for example, Stuart Hall's (2021) discussion on mis/appropriations of Frantz Fanon. On 'un/timeliness' with special reference to ideas from outside of 'known' sources, see Pasha (2011).

Key move: diagnosing IR as a cultural product.

Opening: inquiring into the Eurocentrism of IR as a universalisation of a particular understanding of how the world works.

Closure: exoticisation of 'non-Europe' as an unintended consequence of critical IR's celebration of difference.

Inquiries into IR in Other Parts of the World

Chan and Grovogui's diagnosis of IR as a cultural product was not a part of or in response to IR in other parts of the world. Their books were written when they were located in institutions of higher education in North America and Western Europe. At the same time, both scholars had experience with and background in contexts outside North America and Western Europe, bringing with them a different body of intellectual resources and sensibilities which they cultivated in a manner akin to Said's 'exile as a metaphor' (see Chapter 3).[16] When Chan and Grovogui highlighted the Eurocentric limitations of IR, they were referring to IR as it was practised in North America and Western Europe. IR scholarship from outside these locales did not feature in their discussions, or in the fledgling Postcolonial IR literature. For that, I turn to two studies which inquired into IR around the world, namely Arlene Tickner and Ole Waever's edited volume *International Relations Scholarship Around the World* (2009a) and Amitav Acharya and Barry Buzan's edited volume *Non-Western International Relations Theory: Perspectives on and beyond Asia* (2007).

Let us begin by worlding these two studies, both of which responded to a world of IR that was already worlded by Hoffman's (1977) article. So much so that in the decades that followed the publication of Hoffman's article, scholarly reflections on the state of the field came to portray this eventuality in terms of the 'hegemony' of US IR while at the same time seeking to point to the existence of IR in their own locale, be it the United Kingdom (Smith, 1987), Australia (Kubalkova & Cruickshank, 1987) or Western Europe (Jørgensen, 2000; Waever 1998). As regards the rest of the world, relatively little was known. Consider, for example, a survey volume edited by John Groom and Margot Light (1994) which devoted one chapter to the world outside North America and Western

---

[16] See Chapter 3 for further discussion.

Europe. It was entitled "Beyond North-West: Africa and the East" and was authored by Chan (1994). A previous study edited by Hugh Dyer and Leon Magnasarian (1989) had offered more varied representation, with authors reporting on Brazil, South Africa, Japan, Nigeria, Israel, China, and Hispanic America (editors' own choice of term). What was curious about the latter volume was that scholars from 'non-Europe' reported on the state of IR in their parts of the world, with theoretical themes and debates being covered by authors from 'Europe'. Ali Mazrui's (1989) chapter on nuclear non-proliferation was no exception to this intellectual division of labour insofar as he was offering a 'Third World perspective'.

The two volumes under consideration here were both responding to this eventuality as they inquired into IR in other parts of the world. Tickner and Waever (2009a) spearheaded sociology of science inquiries into IR studies around the world, and helped to popularise inquiries into 'worlding as geocultural situatedness' as a way of addressing IR's limitations (as discussed above).[17] Acharya and Buzan (2007) adopted a more historical sociological approach and foregrounded the category of 'non-Western IR'. Notwithstanding their differences, these two volumes have had a joint outcome: re-framing discussions regarding the limitations of IR in terms of 'Western IR' versus the rest. You will recall that this formulation was initially offered by Chan in the 1990s. Come the 2000s, Chan's characterisation of IR as 'Western' turned out to be 'an idea whose time had come'.

Let me begin with Acharya and Buzan's (2009) edited volume, which was initially published as a special issue of the journal *International Relations of the Asia-Pacific* (Acharya & Buzan, 2007). When introducing the journal special issue Acharya and Buzan first raised the question: "Why is there no non-Western international theory?" Having diagnosed the state of IR outside North America and Western Europe in terms of an 'absence' of theory, the authors asked: Why is it that non-Western scholars, notwithstanding a misfit between Western IR theory and non-Western experiences, have not pursued their own theories? (authors' choice of terms). Surely, Acharya and Buzan suggested, Asian states would be interested in having their own theories to serve their own purposes, and scholars would be expected to rise to the occasion. From 2007 to 2009, when the journal special issue was turned into an edited volume,

[17] Both authors of this book were involved in various aspects of Tickner and Waever's 'geocultural epistemologies' project.

Acharya and Buzan had adjusted the title but nevertheless remained reso-lute in their characterisation of IR in Asia in terms of an 'absence' of theory.[18]

Different from Acharya and Buzan, Tickner and Waever explicitly resisted organising their effort around 'absence' as such. When intro-ducing their study, Tickner and Waever (2009b: 1) noted that surveys of IR beyond North America and Western Europe, when done "without a concrete study of non-dominant and non-privileged parts of the world...become[s] yet another way of speaking from the centre about the whole, and of depicting the centre as normal and the periphery as a projected 'other' through which the disciplinary core is reinforced". Adopting an updated version of the sociology of science approach that Waever had previously utilised,[19] Tickner and Waever (2009b: 1) proposed the following:

> In order to transcend this state of affairs, it is necessary to actually know about the ways in which IR is practised around the world, and to iden-tify the concrete mechanisms shaping the field in distinct geocultural sites, a knowledge effort which must use theories drawn from sociology (and history) of science, postcolonialism, and several other fields.

Their edited volume was a first in its ambition to look at IR studies around the world. In comparison, Acharya and Buzan's volume was not as ambitious, geographically speaking.

One of the important contributions of the Tickner and Waever volume was the way in which it helped to problematise the categories through which IR scholars had previously made sense of the persistence of US hegemony. For instance, Thomas Biersteker's (2009) contribution suggested that the persistence of US hegemony would be better under-stood as an ability to define what is worth publishing in top journals, and not in terms of a particular paradigm as was previously believed (cf. Smith 1987). Biersteker found that those publications also found their way to the reading lists of universities in the US and elsewhere in the world.

---

[18] Acharya and Buzan (2009: 16) did not consider postcolonial studies an 'authentic' alternative to 'Western IR' because, they wrote, "it is basically framed within cultural discourse originating from the West". For further discussion, see Chapter 3.

[19] Waever (1998) had previously engaged in another mapping exercise of journal publications, concluding that IR was a 'not so international' discipline.

Therein rested the roots of US IR's hegemony, concluded Tickner and Waever (2009c: 337), in the "authority over decisions concerning what qualifies as 'theory'".

But then, it seems that we returned to the problem of 'absence', albeit in a roundabout way. What we learned from Tickner and Waever's survey volume was that the "amalgamate" kind of IR that Takashi Inoguchi (2009: 63) observed in Japan was practised in other parts of the world as well. According to Inoguchi (2009: 63), Japan's IR was "like a mosaic with different methodological traditions harmlessly coexisting with each other". According to the author, this made "it more difficult to produce theories for international relations" in Japan. While we do not always take notice of IR in such amalgamated forms, this is because it does not appear in well-known (read: top) outlets. However, one only needs to attend regional IR conferences (as with the Central and Eastern European ISA) or the triannual conference of the World International Studies Committee (WISC) to see how the international is accounted for in such 'amalgamated' form in myriad places.

Revisiting Acharya and Buzan's question in light of their findings, Tickner and Waever (2009c: 339) insisted

Without producing that much of its own IR theory and perspectives, IR 'works' in many places, but this means something markedly different than in the core. Instead of comparing it to IR in the core—and defining peripheral IR in terms of what it is *not*—it is necessary to see what it *is*. To take seriously what IR *does* by doing what it does. Real existing IR in non-privileged parts of the world is a purposeful, meaningful, and socially relevant activity, only under conditions different from those in the core. (emphasis in the original)

However, even as they began with the premise that IR might take multiple forms, Tickner and Waever's answer nevertheless ended up sharing Acharya and Buzan's presumption regarding the 'absence' of theory in other parts of the world. This was not like Hoffman's parochialism preventing him from recognising others' IR as 'IR'. Indeed, the editors of the two volumes explicitly recognised the multiple forms that IR has taken in different parts of the world. This was more akin to Holsti's parochialism which prevented him from recognising others' thinking about world politics as 'theory'.

Remembering the original formulation of Acharya and Buzan's question "Why is there no non-Western IR theory?" as well as Tickner's (2008) observation from an earlier study on the "invisibility" of Third World scholarship (author's choice of term), the question is less about an 'absence' or 'invisibility' and more about IR's obliviousness to scholars from outside Western Europe and North America, argued Shilliam (2011). Such obliviousness is rooted in assumptions that IR shares with other social sciences as to who and what is defined as theorist and theory.

I'll conclude by underscoring how these two volumes worlded the world of IR. Since the publication of these two studies, the questions asked by IR scholars came to focus on worlding the geocultural situatedness of scholars, sociology of science inquiries into the development of IR in different parts of the world, and efforts to theorise from the 'non-West' so as to make up for its purported 'absence'. That is to say, the readers of these two volumes took 'absence' as such at face value.

Key move: inquiring into IR studies around the world.
Opening: adopting an explicitly pluralist stance.
Closure: treating 'non-Western IR' in terms of an 'absence' (albeit in different ways).

Calls for a 'Global IR'

The notion of a 'Global IR' was offered by Amitav Acharya in his capacity as the president of the International Studies Association during 2014–2015. Keeping with our mode of tracing the trajectory of the scholarship in terms of both the situatedness and constitutive power of knowing, let me begin by considering Acharya's presidential address. Its full title was "Global International Relations (IR) and Regional Worlds". Noting the full title is important because the latter part (Regional Worlds) was as central to Acharya's project as was the first (Global IR). This is oftentimes missed by Acharya's critics who have interrogated his notion of 'global' *ad nauseam* to the neglect of the other part of his agenda.[20] Let us also note that Acharya (2014: 649) introduced Global IR as "not a theory, but an aspiration for greater inclusiveness and diversity in our discipline".

[20] But see, Futák-Campbell (2021).

Worlding Acharya's presidential address, two observations are in order. First, as noted above, Acharya's earlier work had embraced a more historical sociological approach. This concern was also visible in the 2014 text. Acharya's previous scepticism regarding Postcolonial Studies, in turn, was replaced by a selective inclusion of Postcolonial IR, most prominently L.H.M. Ling, on whose call for "humility and learning" Acharya (2014: 657) concluded his article. Second, a prominent aspect of Acharya's agenda was regional studies, with his interest in 'Regional Worlds' coming up throughout the article. Put differently, encouraging IR scholars to learn from 'Regional Worlds' was central to Acharya's agenda. In doing so, Acharya was responding to a world of IR that was worlded by Holsti insofar as both authors identified IR's limitations in terms of the absence of voices from outside North America and Western Europe. The point being, Acharya's 'Global IR and Regional Worlds' agenda responded to the normative and analytical dimensions of Eurocentrism. While his writings occasionally acknowledged the epistemological dimension as well, rethinking IR concepts and theories was *not* as central to Acharya's agenda as achieving recognition for 'Regional Worlds' and regional actors' diverse ways of approaching world politics.

Finally, let us consider how Acharya's 'Global IR and Regional Worlds' agenda worlded the world of IR. On the one hand, Acharya put the issue of IR's Eurocentric limitations on the radar of IR scholars around the world. On the other hand, the contributors to the 'Global IR' effort, but perhaps even more so their critics (who tend to focus on a very narrow and selective reading of Acharya's post-2014 work, it has to be said)[21] have fallen into the trap of navel-gazing. While, as noted in Chapter 1, early efforts had emerged from a frustration with conventional and critical IR's inability to make sense of the situation on the ground and therefore had a practical impetus, much of the more recent discussions, especially those who focus exclusively on critiquing Acharya's 2014 article, have failed to link their insights to the practices of international relations–other than theorising, that is. That said, Acharya's call for a 'Global IR' was less a theoretical agenda and more a call for discussion and debate—a call that has been undeniably successful in sheer volume if not always in

---

[21] See, for example, Acharya's critique of Traditional and Critical Security Studies: Acharya (1997, 2000).

substance. Indeed, it is difficult to know for how much longer the above-mentioned critiques of IR's Eurocentric limitations would have remained on the margins of IR if it was not for Acharya's agenda-setting move.

Key move: putting 'Global IR' on the agenda of IR scholars around the world.
Opening: recognition for 'Regional Worlds' and regional actors' their diverse ways of approaching the world.
Closure: willing 'Global IR' into existence via discussions on the state of the discipline even as debates have bifurcated into critiques of global/ity in IR theorising on the one hand, and exploration of regions on the other, with next to no conversation between them.

CONCLUSION

At the time of writing this book, I am cognisant of responding to a world of IR that has been worlded by Acharya's call for a 'Global IR and Regional Worlds', which catapulted concerns with Eurocentrism to the agenda of IR scholars in a previously unforeseen manner. Since then, the literature has developed along multiple axes. Chapter 3 will take stock of available approaches, identifying their strengths and weaknesses toward contributing to (what we call) thinking globally about world politics. Before moving on, let me reiterate that the 'globalising turn' seems to have come to a halt insofar as some of the contributors to recent debates have not only failed to learn from thirty plus years of critical inquiry into the Eurocentric limitations of IR, but have also failed to engage with IR scholars in other parts of the world as coeval thinkers. The irony is not lost on me: those writings that purportedly seek to globalise IR are rarely aware of the scholarship by their contemporaries in other parts of the world, with scholars engaging in navel gazing, or, at best, embarking on their own ethnographic inquiry into different parts of the world as if it is a blank slate (akin to how the Third World was worlded by the colonisers, as discussed by Spivak).

BIBLIOGRAPHY

Acharya, A. (1997). The Periphery as the Core: The Third World and Security Studies. In K. Krause & M. C. Williams (Eds.), *Critical Security Studies: Concepts and Cases* (pp. 299–328). UCL Press.

Acharya, A. (2000). Ethnocentrism and Emancipatory IR Theory. In S. Arnold & J. M. Bier (Eds.), *Displacing Security*. Centre for International and Security Studies, York University.

Acharya, A. (2014). Global International Relations (IR) and Regional Worlds. *International Studies Quarterly, 58*(4), 647–659.

Acharya, A., & Buzan, B. (2007). Why Is There No Non-Western International Relations Theory? An Introduction. *International Relations of the Asia-Pacific, 7*(3), 287–312.

Acharya, A., & Buzan, B. (Eds.). (2009). *Non-Western International Relations Theory: Perspectives on and Beyond Asia*. Routledge.

Agathangelou, A. M., & Ling, L. H. M. (1997). Postcolonial Dissidence Within Dissident IR: Transforming Master Narratives of Sovereignty In Greco-Turkish Cyprus. *Studies In Political Economy, 54*(1), 7–38.

Ahluwalia, P., & Sullivan, M. (2001). Beyond International Relations: Edward Said and the World. In R. A. Crawford & D. S. Jarvis (Eds.), *International Relations—Still an American Social Science? Toward Diversity in International Thought* (pp. 349–367). State University of New York Press.

Alker, H., & Biersteker, T. J. (1984). The Dialectics of World Order: Notes for a Future Archaeologist of International Savoir Faire. *International Studies Quarterly, 28*(2), 121–142.

Ashcroft, B., Griffiths, G., & Tiffin, H. (2009). *Post-Colonial Studies: The Key Concepts* (2nd ed.). Routledge.

Bhambra, G. K. (2007). *Rethinking Modernity: Postcolonialism and the Sociological Imagination*. Palgrave.

Biersteker, T. J. (2009). The Parochialism of Hegemony: Challenges For "American" International Relations. In A. B. Tickner & O. Waever (Eds.), *Global Scholarship in International Relations: Worlding Beyond the West* (pp. 308–327). Routledge.

Bilgin, P. (2008). Thinking Past "Western" IR? *Third World Quarterly, 29*(1), 5–23.

Bilgin, P. (2016). *The International in Security, Security in the International*. Routledge.

Blaney, D. L., & Inayatullah, N. (1994). Prelude To a Conversation of Cultures in International Society? Todorov and Nandy on the Possibility of Dialogue. *Alternatives: Global, Local, Political, 19(1)*, 23–51.

Blaney, D. L., & Tickner, A. B. (2017). Worlding, Ontological Politics and the Possibility of a Decolonial IR. *Millennium: Journal of International Studies, 45*(3), 293–311.

Bleiker, R. (1997). Forget IR Theory. *Alternatives: Global, Local, Political, 22*(1), 57–85.

Chan, S. (1985). China's Foreign Policy and Africa: The Rise and Fall of China's Three World's Theory. *The Round Table, 74*(296), 376–384.

Chan, S. (1994). Beyond North-West: Africa and the East. In A. J. R. Groom & M. Light (Eds.), *Contemporary International Relations: A Guide to Theory* (pp. 237–254). Pinter.

Chan, S. (1996). *Towards A Multicultural Roshamon Paradigm in International Relations: Collected Essays.* Tampere Peace Research Institute.

Chan, S. (2022). *The Lived International: A Life in International Relations.* Rowman and Littlefield.

Chan, S., Mandaville, P. G., & Bleiker, R. (Eds.). (2001). *The Zen of International Relations: IR Theory from East to West.* Palgrave Macmillan.

Darby, P., & Paolini, A. J. (1994). Bridging International Relations and Postcolonialism. *Alternatives, 19*(3), 371–397.

Dyer, H. C., & Mangasarian, L. (Eds.). (1989). *The Study of International Relations: The State of the Art.* Macmillan.

Futák-Campbell, B. (Ed.) (2021). *Globalizing Regionalism and International Relations.* Bristol University Press.

George, J., & Campbell, D. (1990). Patterns of Dissent and the Celebration of Difference: Critical Social Theory and International Relations. *International Studies Quarterly*, 269–293.

Global Society. (2003). Special Issue: Locating the 'I' In 'IR': Dislocating Euro-American Theories. *Global Society, 17*(2).

Groom, A. J. R., & Light, M. (Eds.). (1994). *Contemporary International Relations: A Guide to Theory.* Pinter Publishers.

Grovogui, S. N. (1996). *Sovereigns, Quasi-Sovereigns and Africans: Race and Self-Determination in International Law.* University Of Minnesota Press.

Grovogui, S.N., 2001. Come to Africa: A hermeneutics of race in international theory. *Alternatives, 26*(4), 425–448.

Grovogui, S.N., 2002. Regimes of sovereignty: International morality and the African condition. *European Journal of International Relations, 8*(3), 315–338.

Grovogui, S. N. (2006). *Beyond Eurocentrism and Anarchy: Memories of International Order and Institutions.* Palgrave Macmillan.

Grovogui, S. N. (2013). IR As Theology, Reading Kant Badly, and the Incapacity of Western Political Theory to Travel Very Far In Non-Western Contexts. *Theory Talks*, Retrieved From http://www.theory-talks.org/2013/08/theory-talk-57.html

Guzzini, S. (1993). Structural Power: The Limits of Neorealist Power Analysis. *International Organization, 47*(3), 443–478.

Hall, S. (2021). *Selected Writings on Race and Difference.* Duke University Press.

Hoffman, S. (1977). An American Social Science: International Relations. *Daedalus, 106*(3), 41–60.

Holsti, K. J. (1985). *The Dividing Discipline: Hegemony and Diversity in International Theory*. Allen and Unwin.

Hutchings, K. (2023). Doing Epistemic Justice in International Relations: Women and the History of International Thought. *European Journal of International Relations, 29*(4), 809–831.

Inayatullah, N., & Blaney, D. L. (1996). Knowing Encounters: Beyond Parochialism in International Relations Theory. In Y. Lapid & F. V. Kratochwil (Eds.), *The Return of Culture and Identity in IR Theory* (pp. 65–84). Lynne Rienner Publishers.

Inayatullah, N., & Blaney, D. L. (2004). *International Relations and the Problem of Difference*. Routledge.

Inoguchi, T. (2009). Why are there No Non-Western Theories of International Relations? The Case of Japan. In A. Acharya & B. Buzan (Eds.), *Non-Western International Relations Theory: Perspectives on and Beyond Asia* (pp. 51–68). Routledge.

Jabri, V., & Chan, S. (1996). The Ontologist Always Rings Twice: Two More Stories About Structure and Agency in Reply to Hollis and Smith. *Review Of International Studies, 22*(1), 107–110.

Jørgensen, K. E. (2000). Continental IR Theory: The Best Kept Secret. *European Journal of International Relations, 6*(1), 9–42.

Krishna, S. (1993). The Importance of Being Ironic: A Poscolonial View on Critical International Relations Theory. *Alternatives, 18*(3), 385–417.

Krishna, S. (1999). *Postcolonial Insecurities: India, Sri Lanka, and the Question of Nationhood*. University of Minnesota Press.

Kubalkova, V., & Cruickshank, A. (1987). The Study of International Relations in the South Pacific. *Australian Journal of International Affairs, 41*(2), 110–129.

Kuhn, T. S. (1962). *The Structure of Scientific Revolutions*. University Of Chicago Press.

Ling, L. H. M. (1996). Hegemony and the Internationalizing State: A Post-Colonial Analysis of China's Integration into Asian Corporatism. *Review of International Political Economy, 3*(1), 1–26.

Ling, L. H. M. (2002). The Fish and the Turtle: Multiple Worlds as Method. In M. Brecher & F. P. Harvey (Eds.), *Millennial Reflections on International Studies* (pp. 283–288). The University of Michigan Press.

Mamdani, M., Premesh, L., Walter, D., Mignolo, O. G., Agathangelou, A. M., & Clarke, K. M. (2016). A Discussion on Siba Grovogui's "Beyond Euro-centrism and Anarchy: Memories of International Order and Institutions". *Comparative Studies of South Asia, Africa and the Middle East, 36*(1).

Marlin-Bennett, R. (Ed.). (2012). *Alker and IR: Global Studies in an Interconnected World*. Routledge.

Mazrui, A. A. (1989). The Political Culture of War and Nuclear Proliferation: A Third World Perspective. In H. C. Dyer & L. Mangasarian (Eds.), *The Study of International Relations: The State of the Art* (pp. 155–171). Macmillan.

McGrane, B. (1989). *Beyond Anthropology: Society and the Other*. Columbia University Press.

Muppidi, H. (1999). Postcoloniality and the Production of International Insecurity: The Persistent Puzzle of US-Indian Relations. In J. Weldes, M. Laffey, H. Gusterson, & R. Duvall (Eds.), *Cultures of Insecurity: States, Communities, and the Production Of Danger* (pp. 119–146).

Parmar, I. (2002). American Foundations and the Development of International Knowledge Networks. *Global Networks, 2*(1), 13–30.

Pasha, M. K. (2011). Untimely Reflections. In R. Shilliam (Ed.), *International Relations and Non-Western Thought: Imperialism, Colonialism, and Investigations op Global Modernity* (pp. 217–226). Routledge.

Pasha, M. K. (2017). Religion and the Fabrication of Race. *Millennium: Journal of International Studies, 45*(3), 312–334.

Pettman, J. (1996). *Worlding Women: A Feminist International Politics*. Cambridge University Press.

Shilliam, R. (Ed.). (2011). *International Relations and Non-Western Thought: Imperialism, Colonialism, and Investigations of Global Modernity*. Routledge.

Slater, D. (1998). Post-Colonial Questions for Global Times. *Review of International Political Economy, 5*(4), 647–678.

Smith, S. (1987). Paradigm Dominance in International Relations: The Development of International Relations as a Social Science. *Millennium: Journal of International Studies, 16*(2), 189.

Spivak, G. C. (1985). The Rani of Sirmur: An Essay in Reading the Archives. *History and Theory, 24*(3), 247–272.

Spivak, G. C. (1999). *A Critique of Postcolonial Reason: Toward A History of the Vanishing Present*. Harvard University Press.

Thakur, V., & Smith, K. (2021). Introduction to the Special Issue: The Multiple Births of International Relations. *Review of International Studies, 47*(5), 571–579.

Tickner, A. B. (2008). Aquí En El Ghetto: Hip-Hop in Colombia, Cuba, and Mexico. *Latin American Politics and Society, 50*(3), 121–146.

Tickner, A. B., & Waever, O. (Eds.). (2009). *Global Scholarship in International Relations: Worlding Beyond the West*. Routledge.

Tickner, A. B., & Waever, O. (2009b). Introduction: Geocultural Epistemologies. In A. B. Tickner & O. Waever (Eds.), *International Relations Scholarship Around the World*. Routledge.

Tickner, A. B., & Waever, O. (2009c). Conclusion: Worlding Where the West Once Was. In A. B. Tickner & O. Waever (Eds.), *International Relations Scholarship Around the World*. Routledge.

Trownsell, T., Behera, N. C., & Shani, G. (2022). Introduction to the Special Issue: Pluriversal Relationality. *Review of International Studies, 48*(5), 787–800.

Vitalis, R. (2018). *White World Order, Black Power Politics: The Birth of American International Relations*. Cornell University Press.

Waever, O. (1996). The Rise and Fall of the Inter-Paradigm Debate. In S. Smith, K. Booth, & M. Zalewski (Eds.), *International Theory: Positivism and Beyond* (pp. 149–184). Cambridge University Press.

Waever, O. (1998). The Sociology of a Not So International Discipline: American and European Developments in International Relations. *International Organization, 52*(4), 687–727.

Wight, C. (2012). Philosophy of Social Science and International Relations. In W. Carlsnaes, T. Risse, & B. A. Simmons (Eds.), *Handbook of International Relations* (pp. 29–56). Sage.

CHAPTER 3

Approaches to Thinking Globally About World Politics

Pinar Bilgin and Karen Smith

Abstract This chapter asks how to start the process of doing research that addresses Eurocentrism in International Relations (IR). It begins by recognising that, when thinking globally about world politics, a major obstacle facing us is a failure to be puzzled, because we presume that we already understand. One of the first steps, therefore, is learning to be *genuinely* puzzled, for which we can turn to strategies employed by scholars like Said. The rest of the chapter takes stock of available approaches to thinking globally about world politics, which are presented according to their place on a continuum of connectedness in the way they understand the production of ideas and knowledge about how the world works. These include worlding as geocultural situatedness, non-Western IR, worlding, everyday IR, decentring, historical connections, relationality, contrapuntal reading, and constitutive outside.

Keywords Exile as method · Contrapuntal reading · Relationality · Worldism · Geocultural situatedness · Non-Western IR · Everyday · Decentring · Connectedness · Constitutive outside

Introduction

While an increasing number of scholars recognise the importance of engaging in research that addresses IR's Eurocentrism, they often get stuck when faced with the question of how exactly they are going to go about doing this. It is easy to feel overwhelmed at the thought that what we have come to know as IR is based on a very limited understanding of the world, and that the research tools that we are familiar with are perhaps not sufficient for the purposes of thinking globally about world politics. This is both exciting—think about the tremendous opportunities this opens up—and intimidating. Where do we even begin?

Oftentimes, this is a practical concern. For scholars trained in conventional or even critical IR, considering new ways of doing research, and learning to use new research tools can seem quite daunting. Sometimes such resistance could also be about attempts at disciplining those who introduce new research tools that are coupled with different epistemologies, ontologies, and/or methodologies. As Roland Bleiker (2017: 260) noted, "[o]pening up thinking space inevitably involves risks. It is to embrace creativity, and the uncertainty associated with it, over the comfort of time-honoured procedures and disciplinary conventions." Unavoidably, questions about what constitutes 'knowledge' and how to produce it are raised. Indeed, addressing Eurocentrism requires us to challenge an assumption that lies at its heart, namely the idea that only 'Europe'[1] has proven capable of producing 'knowledge', whilst treating other ways of knowing as 'less than'.[2]

Different approaches to research are not independent of individual scholars' experiences of the international.[3] For example, as an Indigenous scholar, Linda Tuhiwai-Smith (2021b) foregrounded the importance of recognising Indigenous knowledge and Indigenous ways of knowing. When Edward Said (1984) proposed that we think through exile as a 'metaphorical condition' (see below) he was reflecting on his own experiences as a Palestinian who was not able to return home. Some researchers may be drawn to particular approaches based on their past training and

---

[1] In our use, 'Europe' refers to the birthplace of Eurocentrism, and includes both North America and Western Europe. See Chapter 1 for further discussion.

[2] For an elaborate discussion from a Feminist perspective, see Harding (1991). For a more recent discussion in the IR context, see Shilliam (2014).

[3] See the Postscript for further discussion.

familiarity with certain ways of doing research. Others may prefer a specific approach because of their discomfort with their past training, as with Hayward Alker (1996: 148) who, in his presidential address to the 1992 annual convention of the International Studies Association, remarked how "[t]he positivistic exploratory approaches of my early research now appear inadequate for addressing such challenging reorderings of both space, time and human lives", and that "my preliminary epistemological map of the (inter-) disciplinary world of International Relations research has proven to be too small by a third". Positionality matters, but it is not the only thing that matters. As discussed in Chapter 2, IR and ir[4] have worlded us all even as we seek to push back against the limits of what and how we can know about the international.

As Tuhiwai-Smith (2021a, 2021b: 43) reminded us, "the methodologies and methods of research, the theories that inform them, the questions which they generate and the writing styles they employ, all become significant acts which need to be considered carefully and critically before being applied." Some think this is because methods are the 'Master's tools', as Audre Lorde (2012 [1984]) characterised it, insofar as they have served the interests of those who put 'Europe' at the centre of the study of world politics. Does it, then, make sense to utilise those very methods when seeking to think globally about world politics?

We think it depends. For one thing, labelling some research tools as 'Master's tools' means giving into the 'Master's narrative' about the 'European origin' of ideas and things. Those 'scientific' methods that are portrayed as having originated in 'Europe' have surprisingly complex lineages that belie such linear narratives. Furthermore, such presumptions contradict our Saidian premise (see below) that ideas do not have a single origin but rather multiple beginnings.

This is not to dismiss the concerns behind the historical utilisation of methods by the powerful against the powerless. "For the native, objectivity is always directed against him", wrote thinker Franz Fanon (quoted in Said, 2000b: 98). Said (2000b: 98) empathised with Fanon's frustration insofar as "native literature" has been portrayed to be "of a place rather than coeval contributions to knowledge", he wrote. But then, while

---

[4] We use ir as a shorthand for world politics, while remaining sensitive to the distinctions scholars make between the study of world politics versus international relations.

some methods have served the powerful, they have also been utilised by the powerless to rebel against the powerful.[5]

There is an additional difficulty when trying to avoid so-called 'Master's tools' and searching for alternatives in other places. That is, we may not have the necessary training to make sense of them. There is a "danger", Stephen Chan (2017: viii) wrote, when "a vast array of 'other' thought is suddenly paraded by progressive International Relations scholars who are not linguists, theologians, or who have never been near the locales where they source their new 'thought'". Not to mention the hubris involved in presuming that we can make sense of, say, Fanon or Spivak by reading only one article or book chapter, let alone ancient texts by ancient scholars. Taking such a step is especially problematic if it is done by overlooking the rich literature produced by scholars who have spent their lifetimes doing exactly that. In other words, there is no easy way out.

This chapter will take stock of available approaches to thinking globally about world politics, including scholarship that developed through thirty plus years of addressing IR's Eurocentric limitations as well as their reincarnation as part of the so-called 'globalising turn'.[6] Here is where we stand: there is not just one way of thinking globally about world politics. Instead, we should be open to multiple and at times interlocking strategies that problematise narratives and subjects.[7] Our stance seems to be shared by some of the scholars interviewed for the Postscript. Kevin Dunn says, "I don't think there is a way. I think one assaults hegemony in as many ways as one can…I wouldn't want to close off any possibilities of counter-hegemonic practices." Siddharth Mallavarapu shares this view, contending "I think there's no one size fits all here, really. And I think different scholars should take a jab at it with what they're most comfortable with." That said, as co-authors, we each have our own preferred approaches, as will become clear later on in the chapter.

---

[5] Also see the Postscript for further discussion.

[6] We use 'globalising turn' to refer to the effort spearheaded by Amitav Acharya since 2014. The body of scholarship seeking to address IR's Eurocentric limitations has a much longer history.

[7] Please note that this is not the same as Rudra Sil and Peter Katzenstein's (2010) call for eclecticism when choosing research tools. While we are not against 'analytic eclecticism' per se, we insist that the issues we face run deeper than that. For further discussion, see below.

While an exhaustive discussion of methodology and methods falls beyond the scope of this chapter, we tried to be as comprehensive as possible in our discussion of different approaches that you might find useful in deciding where to begin. As noted above, this is not to give up on questions of methodology and methods; rather, we encourage students of world politics to reflect on the limitations of what they have at hand, including the structural constraints that they function within, and consider alternatives that are available to them. Our thinking is that reflecting on methodology and methods begins when a research question is being formulated. We proceed with two separate but related discussions on learning to be puzzled and looking differently.

Learning to be Puzzled

When thinking globally about world politics, a major obstacle facing us is a failure to be puzzled, because we presume that 'we already understand' (Bilgin, 2016). Reflecting on the benefits of estrangement, Siddharth Mallavarapu says,

> It's a good place to be in, and I think we should all for a while suspend our familiar assumptions about things around us. ...I think it's wonderful to be in our fields of study, where we are constantly challenged by a complex world. It's befuddling. It's a good thing that it's befuddling, because the moment we cease to think it's befuddling I think we're back to platitudes and certitudes which are not good scholarship. They're just sort of lulling us into some sort of misplaced understanding of the world.[8]

Indeed, over the years, students of world politics time and again failed to acknowledge the limits of their theorising even as their concepts and categories fell short of capturing the phenomena they encountered. Examples abound, but consider the following: the persistence of the state of Lebanon even as it has given up the monopoly of legitimate use of violence; the way India, throughout the 1960s, refused to practise deterrence in the way it was anticipated from a nuclear power, and insisted on its 'postcolonial bomb'; the shock expressed by the US and EU when their stance vis-à-vis Russia's war against Ukraine was not supported in the same manner by many African leaders, among others; the apparent

---

[8] See the Postscript for more on this.

inexplicability of South Africa's wavering position on LGBTQI+ rights at the UN.[9] Students of IR have responded to these instances by seeking to fit them into their existing frameworks, or explaining them away by filing them away as failures, short-termist pragmatism or even irrationality. Something is wrong with them; surely, not with our concepts and theories! In fact, all of these examples are potential starting points for research projects—if only we were sufficiently puzzled.

On the one hand, thinking in terms of puzzles is a recognised way of thinking theoretically about world politics. We call those phenomena 'puzzles' which we fail to explain using our existing concepts, categories and theories. On the other hand, what is tricky about identifying puzzles, particularly when thinking globally about world politics, is our past training: we are accustomed to thinking that 'we already understand' notwithstanding contrasting evidence, at times. Therefore, oftentimes we fail to be puzzled by those instances that do not quite fit our concepts and theories. We offer accounts that almost explain but not quite, without feeling intellectually disconcerted. That is to say, being puzzled and looking differently are skills that need acquiring when thinking globally about world politics.

To renounce the fiction that 'we already understand' and to learn to be puzzled, in this book we turn to Said's approach to 'exile as metaphor'. Without underestimating the taxing situation that people who are in exile find themselves in, Said appreciated the exile's ability to have a plurality of vision. Such "eccentricity" allows the exile not only "the negative advantage of refuge," wrote Said, but also "the positive benefit of challenging the system, describing it in language unavailable to those it has already subdued" (Said, 1993: 334). For Said himself, being in exile was both his life experience and a "metaphorical condition" (Morefield, 2022).[10] In his writings, Said explored the works of other authors that were produced when in exile, learning from their reflections and offering

---

[9] But see, Hazbun (2016), Abraham (1998), Grovogui (2023) respectively, on Lebanon, India, and African responses to Russian aggression toward Ukraine. On South African foreign policy, see Chapter 5.

[10] Exile was a life experience for Said, because his family had to leave their homeland in Palestine and was never able to return. Said was educated in Egypt and later the United States, becoming a professor of English and Comparative Literature at Columbia University. In various works, Said (1999) reflected on his loss of home, and existence between two worlds as a Palestinian and an American (by virtue of his father's US citizenship gained through military service).

'exile as metaphor'. Building on his own experiences and those of others, Said argued that while "most people are principally aware of one culture, one setting, one home; exiles are aware of at least two, and this plurality of vision gives rise to an awareness of simultaneous dimensions, an awareness that—to borrow a phrase from music—is contrapuntal" (Said, 2000a: 199).

We will further explore contrapuntal reading later in the chapter. Suffice it to note here that through exploring 'exile as metaphor', Said reminded his readers of the need to stop making do with simplifications and to learn how to be comfortable in a "loss of comfort", how to stop mourning for the "loss of surety" and open ourselves to being puzzled. Here, it is also important to acknowledge the work of feminist and queer theorists who contend that we should reject the goal of simplifying the world and categorising it (often in binary terms) in order to discipline it and rid it of any contradictions and ambiguities; and that we should allow for 'both/and', and not just 'either/or' (Weber, 2015). This sense of being out of place, experiencing a sense of puzzlement, or discomfort, or looking in from the margins (whether geographically, disciplinarily or otherwise) is something all the scholars interviewed for the Postscript mention explicitly or implicitly. Said's call for puzzlement was about turning such discomfort with 'both/and' into a research agenda (Morefield, 2022). The goal, then, is not to seek to overcome discomfort, but to think through it.

'Exile as metaphor' is sometimes portrayed as innate to a certain positionality. This is not the case. In this sense, Said's idea is different from "border thinking", an approach originally offered by Gloria Anzaldúa and later developed by Walter Mignolo (2013). Whereas Anzaldúa had emphasised thinking done by those who have previously been left outside through colonial matrices of power (Mayblin, n.d.), Mignolo offered 'border thinking' as characteristic of the Third World. But then, as Uma Narayan (2004) maintained, such arguments that grant 'epistemic advantage' to some people are vulnerable to reification insofar as they tie positionality to innate characteristics. Indeed, Manuela Boatcă's (2015) analysis of intellectuals in Central and Eastern Europe (who have also existed between East/West, First/Second worlds) showed that 'border thinking' is not inherently a reflexive critical practice. Elaborating on this point, Boatcă (2015: 139) approvingly cited Enrique Dussel's caution that the in-between position of living on the border of the East and West or First and Second worlds "implies a significant degree of blindness to full-fledged coloniality". Dussel (1993) was not without hope, however, in that he also saw 'an epistemic potential'. It is up to the immigrant or exile to make something of this potential with a view to its ethical implications, he suggested.

The point is that 'exile as metaphor' is not about positionality, but what we make of it. As students of world politics, we need to learn to reflect to be able to see our limitations. Those limitations may be generated by our positionality, but learning to reflect on our positionality is only a first step. Said's 'exile as metaphor' is about turning reflection into a scholarly reflex so that we do not presume to 'already understand', learn to be puzzled, and ask unsettling questions about the structures that sustain prevalent presumptions. In this book, we advocate Said's approach to 'exile as metaphor' to avoid reification as cautioned by Narayan, and to explore the potential highlighted by Dussel.

Looking Differently

If one of the aims of thinking globally about world politics is to uncover how people in different parts of the world have thought about questions of world politics—in other words, looking for what is already there but has been silenced, co-opted or overlooked—we need to rethink how we go about doing the work, as noted above. Indeed, if we are committed to engaging with difference in the sense of recognizing that there are multiple ways of experiencing, thinking about, and doing the international, then we need to be open to different ways of knowing the world. It requires us, in essence, to look in a different way, and to look in different places other than where, as IR scholars, we would normally look. While research methods textbooks can be helpful in setting out guidelines and alerting us to some of the decisions we have to make when undertaking a research project, they often imply that it is a linear process, where we identify a problem, we develop a research question, and on that basis, we choose a methodology, which in turn determines which sources we will employ. Instead, if we start, for example, by looking differently and allow ourselves to imagine utilising different sources, this could lead us to research topics and questions that we would not previously have been able to consider.

Looking differently entails both new research tools, but also using the research tools we are familiar with in different ways. Importantly, while looking differently calls for us to be innovative and creative, it does not mean that we have to start from scratch. There are many available research tools, both from within IR and outside of it, that we can draw on in thinking globally about world politics. We can start by looking outside of established and accepted IR methodologies and methods to those used by historians, sociologists, anthropologists, literary and art scholars. That said, while it is tempting to borrow tools from other disciplines, this brings its own challenges. Some of these disciplines have their own problematic histories that they have also been grappling with. Nevertheless, there is much mutual learning to be done across disciplines, if one remains aware of both the challenges and the lessons learned. This is especially so as IR has been quite late coming to the party of recognising its limitations inherent to Eurocentrism. We can also utilise the progress made in IR through developments like the historical and aesthetic turns and applying these toward thinking globally about world politics.

Looking differently includes thinking differently about sources. While the ultimate decision about sources will of course also be driven by the chosen research tools (for example, visual or textual discourse analysis) early decisions—sometimes implicit—about which sources matter are very much methodologically bounded. Historical archives are an underutilised but rich source of information that has formed the basis of much of the recent work questioning IR's myth of origins (Davis et al., 2020; Vitalis, 2018). There is a vast amount of material available, and historians—particularly global historians—have already done much of the excavation work. In drawing on archives, however, we should also be sensitive to what we regard as 'legitimate' archival sources. Anna Agathangelou (2016: 206) has reminded us of the importance of tapping into "[l]iving archives, as opposed to official documented history, which often denies the stories of people contesting the official version of history". She encouraged us to take a "broader understanding of archives in world politics" to include texts that speak to marginalised knowledge to "living sources of worldviews and expressions of life", recognizing that all of these are "part of international knowledge" (Agathangelou, 2016: 207; also see Shilliam, 2014). In those instances where archives might not exist, it could be up to the researcher to create these–through conducting interviews, for example (also see, El-Malik & Kamola, 2017).

In the field of IR, as in many other social sciences, there is a strong emphasis on written, text-based sources, and in particular peer-reviewed literature. In many societies, there is however an oral rather than a written history tradition, and histories "are stored within genealogies, within the landscape, within weavings and carvings, even within the personal names that many people carried" (Smith, 2021b: 36). Consider also the role of ancestral knowledge in many societies, or the fact that in some Indigenous knowledge traditions dreams constitute a legitimate source of knowledge (Beier, 2005). We must be careful not to think in terms of binaries (rational/irrational, scientific/unscientific) that some knowledge has the status of 'knowledge' and others do not.[11] This is part of the trap of Eurocentrism.

Aesthetic sources can provide insights into ways of thinking about, experiencing, performing and shaping the international that have not (or cannot) be captured by scholarly texts. While training in how to access non-textual sources is not generally part of IR curricula, considerable progress has been made in recent years in the field with regard to rethinking the sources that we can utilise if we want to gain a deeper understanding of international relations. The aesthetic and related visual turn, for example (see Bleiker, 2017, 2018) have challenged the prioritisation of written text, arguing that aesthetic sources are not only important as alternative lenses to understand IR, but they allow us to recognise that international relations is also enacted and performed through various visual media like popular culture. These developments have paved the way for thinking differently about 'legitimate' sources. They also mean that we may have to retool ourselves to become more adept at working with different sources. Driving home the point that looking differently sometimes literally entails looking, in their study of everyday peace photography in Colombia and Brazil, Frank Möller and David Shim (2019) explored the connection between visual images and peace, thereby highlighting local visions of peace as sites of the international. Julia Gallagher (2022) foregrounded architecture in Africa to explore questions of statehood and state-society relations. Drawing on aesthetic theory, she established a new ethnography of statehood through architecture, asking how statehood and sovereignty are understood in the ways citizens use, view and engage with the buildings of the state.

None of this is to suggest that we put aside thirty plus years of effort within IR dedicated to addressing IR's Eurocentric limitations which more recently has amounted to a globalising turn. Nor is it to

---

[11] Another issue to be mindful of is that some embrace their spirituality as part of the attempt to assert their difference toward gaining some agency in (world) politics. For a discussion, see Bilgin and Çapan (2021).

forego the writings of scholars from outside North America and Western Europe by delving directly into ethnography ourselves. In other words, our embrace of the study of the international through thinking differently about sources is not to be viewed as ignorant of the study of world politics by scholars hailing from and or located outside 'Europe'. Put in practical terms, we suggest that before embarking on interviews, for example, it is crucial to make sure that you have exhausted the existing scholarship, especially that of scholars and thinkers whose writings may not be published in 'known outlets' of IR and/or may not always be immediately recognisable as IR. Thinking globally about world politics entails being mindful to treat scholars around the world as coeval thinkers and not as mere sources.

TAKING STOCK OF EXISTING APPROACHES

The rest of the chapter will take stock of existing approaches to thinking globally about world politics. They are presented in terms of our understanding of their place on a continuum of connectedness (from the less to the more) in the way they understand the production of ideas and knowledge about how the world works. We understand 'connectedness' as an umbrella term, comprising the study of 'connected histories', 'interconnectedness', entanglements, and 'enmeshment'. We recognise that these terms are sometimes used interchangeably by scholars who may not always be attentive to their different ontological commitments. We also note that not all of these approaches are focused on the production of ideas and knowledge about how the world works. In what follows, we sidestep this terminological jumble in favour of offering our own understanding of the sort of connectedness entailed in each of the approaches we discuss. In addition, in discussing the different approaches, we keep in mind our definition of thinking globally as involving curiosity about what others think about the world, making sustained effort to locate their thoughts and recognising past and present contributions to what we otherwise view as 'European' ideas, practices, and institutions.

Our own understanding is best captured by Said's distinction between 'origin' versus 'beginnings' of ideas.[12] Whereas looking for the 'origin' of ideas assumes a singular source (for, say, human rights or democracy),

---

[12] The authors would like to thank Zeynep Gülşah Çapan for helping to clarify this point.

an exploration of 'beginnings' takes as its starting point the eventuality that there exist multiple sources across time and space, and focuses on the study of relations of give-and-take and learning between the world's peoples. Following Said (1975: xvii) "beginning is *making* or *producing difference*; but…difference which is the result of combining the already-familiar with the fertile novelty of human work in language" [original emphasis].[13] As with Said, we understand 'the already-familiar' not to be bounded by geoculture (see below).

As with any analytical framework, this represents our attempt at categorising the different approaches without suggesting that this is the only way of doing so, or that distinctions between the different categories are hard and fast. Needless to say, some of the scholars mentioned might disagree with our characterisation. Finally, it should also be noted that many authors, including us, have shifted between different approaches over time. This is also reflected in the discussions with scholars in the Postscript.[14]

Before we proceed, a practical note is in order: If you are in doubt where to locate a particular approach in our continuum of connectedness, consider, as a rule of thumb, how they would understand Said's notion of 'travelling theory' (Bilgin, 2021b). Those who ask the 'does theory travel?' question are located in the former half of our continuum, for they presume concepts and theories originate in one place and then make their way elsewhere. Those who explore multiple beginnings of ideas, practices and institutions across time and space are located in the latter half of our continuum. Our predilections rest with the latter half, as will become apparent in the next two chapters, when we turn to our own individual foci on (international) security (Chapter 4) and foreign policy (Chapter 5).

---

[13] One aspect of the distinction Said makes between 'origin' and 'beginning' is the former being sacred and the latter being secular, but not only that. For a discussion on this aspect and its centrality for Said's humanism, see Morefield (2022: 100–106).

[14] Kevin Dunn, for example, notes how his thinking about how to go about addressing Eurocentrism has changed over time: "I used to think we have to ignore all of the mainstream theories. But that's not where I am now. I think that further marginalises conversations with people who might dismiss us anyway".

'Non-Western IR'

The first approach that we will consider is 'non-western IR', the assumption behind which is that it is possible and desirable to develop a theory of world politics outside of 'Western IR'. The label itself promises much insofar as it zeroes in on 'Westernness' as the source of IR's limitations.[15] Yet, as will be seen, what those scholars who identify with 'non-western IR' have offered thus far is a mixed bag.

Debates about producing 'non-Western' approaches to IR have their origins in the late 1980s in China's local debates.[16] The first step in building a Chinese school of IR was taken when the idea of developing an 'IR theory with Chinese characteristics' was raised. In the absence of a consensus as to how to proceed, not much progress was made at the time. Such efforts were resumed in the 2000s, in a context shaped by global interest in China as a rising power. At the time, Chinese scholars' efforts were embraced by those taking part in the debates that were fuelled by Acharya and Buzan's (2007) polemical question: 'Why is there no non-Western IR theory?' It was in this context of renewed interest in the state of theorising about the international outside North America and Western Europe that a debate that was previously conducted exclusively in Chinese became international (Chan, 1999; cf. Qin, 2013). One takeaway here is that even efforts to disconnect from the centre, as with 'non-Western IR', cannot be understood entirely independently of the rest of IR.[17]

Considering what 'IR theory with Chinese characteristics' has on offer is helpful in illustrating how some approaches to 'non-Western IR' occlude the very avenues they are supposed to open. This is because they

---

[15] 'Post-Western IR' also identifies the 'Westernness' of IR as a limitation but offers to address it not through excluding but by moving beyond 'Western IR'. See, for example, Blaney and Inayatullah (2008), Shani (2008). The scholars who have referred to 'post-Western IR' in their works are covered below under 'worlding as (geocultural) situatedness'.

[16] This is not to overlook other efforts to decolonise knowledge production and teaching of the international. See, for example, Thomas Tieku (2021), on the Legon School. Rather, we're focusing on explicit attempts to construct a 'non-Western IR' understood as not only different but also distinct from what is understood as 'Western IR'. On the decolonial versus postcolonial distinction, see Chapter 1.

[17] To utilise the conceptual vocabulary introduced in Chapter 2, aspirations to have a 'non-Western IR' can only be understood by worlding it in terms of both geocultural situatedness and the constitutive power of knowing.

understand the critique of Eurocentrism only in terms of its normative dimension, and as a derivative of what they presume to be IR's geocultural origin in 'Europe'. They thereby underestimate its comprehensiveness and persistence, which are by-products of the analytical and epistemological dimensions of Eurocentrism. Tied to this narrow interpretation of Eurocentrism is the attempt to replace 'Europe' with another site, which amounts to producing knowledge that is still "linked to a fixed site of irreducible knowledge claims" while reproducing "an ontology that ties knowledge to a location as a singular and essential quality of place" (Abraham, 2006: 210). Such claims to nurture (ostensibly) 'non-Western' sites of knowledge production "end up reproducing and reinforcing the national scale over all others, since these are not debates over science, but always about something else" (Abraham, 2006: 211)—that something else being politics (domestic and international). If this sounds familiar, remember that this is also how Eurocentric knowledge was produced.

Beyond China, failing to address multiple facets of Eurocentrism and reducing it to presumptions of geocultural origin alone, has resulted in a search for quick remedies, as with locating "the most exotic forms of politics around the world and [revelling] in their alien-ness" (Shilliam, 2021: 11). The problem with such attempts, as Robbie Shilliam (2021: 11) noted, is that, "in doing so, you'd keep the 'familiar' familiar and the 'unfamiliar' unfamiliar…No question raised as to what counts as 'exotic' to whom and why". What is more, as Antonio Vázquez-Arroyo (2018: 64) argued, "distance and difference are frequently overstated, sometimes reified, occasionally even concocted". The point about thinking globally about world politics is questioning what such claims to 'difference' render invisible while at the same time avoiding relying upon reifications such as 'Western IR' and 'non-Western IR'.

We place 'non-Western IR' at one end of our continuum of connectedness insofar as it has preserved the Eurocentric edifice of IR—save for its claim to relevance across space. Contra Acharya (2014), the problem here is not that IR concepts and theories are "for the most part derived from the Western context", but that they are derived from a very particular narrative about that context—a narrative that brought 'Europe' into being as an "imaginary entity" (Chakrabarty, 2000). As discussed in Chapter 2 and will be further explored in Chapter 4, this is a narrative that not only gets other parts of the world wrong, it also gets 'Europe' wrong. The point being, if the concepts and theories that draw on this particular narrative are not helpful—neither in 'Europe' nor elsewhere in the world—all our theories and concepts need rethinking, all around the world.

Worlding as (Geocultural) Situatedness

Worlding as a method was re-introduced to IR in Arlene Tickner and Ole Waever's (2009a) edited volume entitled *International Relations Scholarship Around the World*. Our task as IR scholars, Tickner and Waever (2009b: 10) argued, should be one of exploring the ways in which "the field is constituted by numerous intersecting academic practices that are all about the world and all making their own worlds". As discussed in Chapter 2, there are two distinct approaches to worlding. One is about locating ourselves in the world as IR scholars and reflecting on the 'situatedness of knowledge'. Over the years students of critical IR have contributed to worlding in this first sense, by making room for others' approaches to IR. Nevertheless, critical IR's appreciation of others' contributions to and contestations over knowledge has also been found wanting by their critics insofar as they were seen as failing to engage in worlding in the second sense of the term—that is 'worlding as constitutive' of knowledge (which is the second approach introduced in Chapter 2).[18]

Tickner and Waever's (2009a) survey of IR scholarship in different parts of the world was an exploration of worlding in terms of the geocultural situatedness of IR scholars and their scholarship. The authors introduced the notion of 'geocultural epistemologies', highlighting the need to study the nexus of "pioneering cultural analyses of Ali Mazrui...to works emerging from post-colonialism and feminism on the role of geocultural factors in molding epistemological perspectives" (Tickner & Waever, 2009b: 3). Responding to the editors' invitation, the participants of the 'geocultural epistemologies' project offered surveys of the discipline in their corners of the world; writings which showed that those concepts and theories as introduced in 'standard' IR textbooks are also the core concepts of IR scholars in many other parts of the world.

Reflecting on the workshop contributions, Pinar Bilgin (2008) suggested that scholars also inquire into the ways in which IR scholarship seems to be similar—or 'almost the same but not quite', drawing

---

[18] This is not the only criticism levelled against critical IR's response to its Eurocentric limitations, as discussed in Chapter 2.

on Homi Bhabha. Bilgin suggested that what comes across as 'similar' at first sight may turn out to be unexpectedly 'different' or rather, 'differently different' (also see, Bilgin, 2012)—if only we learn to be puzzled and look differently. In the concluding chapter of the 2009 edited volume, Tickner and Waever (2009c: 338) responded by noting that "the prevalent notion that non-core, non-Western readings of International Relations are essentially 'different' needs to be thought through".

The implication of this argument for our discussion is that 'worlding as (geocultural) situatedness' fails to capture how our 'differently different' ways of approaching the international have come about: in other words, as a product of and response to IR's and ir's[19] worlding of the world, including scholars' agency. This is also why we locate 'worlding as (geocultural) situatedness' as an approach only a couple of steps removed from 'non-Western IR' on our continuum of connectedness.

'Worlding as constitutive' entails reflecting on the ways in which IR and ir have worlded us all.[20] In the post-WWII era, doing IR as it has been done in the United States emerged as a way of signalling a break with the past and embracing 'modern-day' ways of doing things in some other parts of the world (Bilgin, 2008; Chen, 2012). In Turkey, for instance, many scholars appropriated concepts and theories of US IR in an attempt to locate themselves in the 'West' (Bilgin, 2012). In the post-Cold War context, Central and East European scholars who wanted to put some distance between themselves and the Cold War past (Drulák, 2009), and Taiwanese and South Korean scholars who sought to distinguish their approaches from China exhibited similar concerns (Seo & Cho, 2021).

While inviting scholars from different parts of the world to reflect on their situatedness has allowed us to see how their ideas were shaped by their context, it has not allowed appreciating the complex dynamics between multiple actors in shaping the study of IR in different parts of the world. Following up on the discussion on positionality (see above), reflecting on our situatedness has to be coupled with considering the ways in which our context has already shaped and been shaped by the world (of IR and ir).

---

[19] Throughout the book, we use ir as a shorthand for world politics, while remaining sensitive to the distinctions some scholars make between the study of world politics versus international relations.

[20] See Chapter 2 for a discussion.

Indeed, worlding the very notion of 'geoculture' is revealing insofar as it presumes geographies and cultures to be pre-given, without considering the ways in which they, too, have been worlded. Let us break it down into its components, geography and culture. To begin with geography, geo-graphing has always been tied up with colonisation at the local and global level. It is in this sense that Said (1978: 55) referred to "imaginative geographies" in so far as what is known about far-away lands "is more than anything else imaginative". And, imagination as such is never independent of power. This is not to say that all knowledge about geography is imaginary, but that "[a]lmost from earliest times in Europe the Orient was something more than what was empirically known about it" (Said, 1978: 55). Replace 'Europe v. the Orient' with any other power relationship, and you encapsulate the complex histories of geography.

The study of culture, the other component of 'geocultural', is no less troubled by its complex history. With the founding of Anthropology as a discipline in the nineteenth century, the study of 'the Other' went through a transformation. No longer approached as 'demonic' as in the sixteenth century, or 'ignorant' as during the Renaissance and Enlightenment, 'the Other's 'cultural difference' became the subject of study. Correspondingly, to quote Bernard McGrane (1989: 94), "Anthropology fossilised difference; it saw difference as fossilisation". The point here is not that this is all that the study of culture has been or can be. It is rather about how Anthropology had its start: as "the modern West's monologue about 'alien cultures'", which has also plagued other disciplines like IR that have borrowed from it without necessarily reflecting on the complex histories involved.

Relatedly, the subsequent calls for geocultural pluralism in IR (which were inspired but not necessarily sanctioned by Tickner and Waever's 'geocultural epistemologies' project)[21] have sought to collect perspectives on the international from different parts of the world, which is akin to approaching "the world as exhibition" (Mitchell, 1989) as "a thing to be viewed", but not necessarily engaging with scholars as coeval producers of knowledge. Remembering that failure to engage with Postcolonial Studies critics was also a limitation for critical IR,[22] let us underscore the following: embracing a plurality of approaches can only help to address

---

[21] See a forum on geocultural pluralism in IR, edited by de Koeijer and Shilliam (2021).
[22] See Chapter 2.

the limitations of IR if it entails questioning ourselves—that is, going beyond professing openness to multiple ontologies and epistemologies for someone else to pursue even as we carry on with business-as-usual. Following Daniel Levine and David McCourt (2018: 103) "pluralism matters, not because of what it adds to our understanding of world politics, but because of what it takes away".

Everyday International

Feminist and Postcolonial Studies scholars in particular have called for including the voiceless, the unheard, those who appear to have limited agency, in constructing accounts of the international. In order to challenge prevalent narratives of the international, they argue, stories must be told from the ground up, from the experience of ordinary people, of those engaged in the day-to-day practice of the international. Such an approach also entails challenging the way the international is regarded as "a zone set apart from the domestic and the personal" (Darby, 2006: 11), and recognises that in order to uncover the international in all its facets, we must look towards, and take seriously, silences and absences, which includes the local and the marginalised. These calls go back to the 1980s, when feminist scholars called for grounded research rooted in situated knowledge.[23] The "everyday life" of international relations (Björkdahl et al., 2019; Enloe, 2011) has since become a rich source of information about how what we sometimes think of as abstract questions (sovereignty, anarchy) play out at the grassroots level. In an article on everyday life across borders in southern Africa, Karen Smith (2021a) showed how borders are experienced less as a marker between inside and outside, us and them, domestic and international, and more a bureaucratic obstacle of little consequence. This suggests that the international operates at different levels, in a fragmented way that draws into question the assumed universality of "commonsense" IR concepts, and their continued relevance for understanding the world in all its diversity and complexity. Accessing the everyday necessitates that IR scholars consider adopting methods more often associated with disciplines like Sociology and Anthropology. While ethnographic methods have become increasingly popular in IR, Wanda

---

[23] See, for example, Harding (1987). For more recent work see, Harding (2004) and Ackerly and True (2010).

Vrasti's caution about the dangers of a selective and instrumental adoption of ethnographic methods by IR scholars is worth repeating here. In particular, Vrasti (2008: 280) lamented the fact that IR has not sufficiently engaged with debates within Anthropology about ethnographic methods, pointing to a "delay in cross-disciplinary reading practice". This is an important point to keep in mind when borrowing methods from other disciplines, as discussed above.

An IR scholar who has engaged with the politics of everyday life, visuality and feminist theory in a thoughtful and reflective manner is Sophie Harman (2019). In her work, Harman explores questions of global health in the African context, including through the use of narrative feature film as a "method of seeing and being seen" (2019: 13) She shows how film as a method can help us to see individuals whose experience of the international is mostly overlooked, and can provide us with alternative insights into matters of world politics such as the securitization of global health, development priorities, and global power dynamics.

Echoing the discussion above (on 'worlding as [geocultural] situatedness'), a cautionary note about searching for 'difference' in the study of the everyday is due here. While a recognition of the heterogeneity of the world and epistemological differences is undoubtedly an important part of thinking globally about world politics, difference should not be overemphasised. It is important to make a distinction between, on the one hand, recognising different ways of thinking about how the world works and, on the other, establishing hierarchies between what are viewed as incommensurable approaches to the international. Scholars like Uma Narayan (1998) and Achille Mbembe (2002) already cautioned about the dangers of over-emphasising difference to the extent that it results in cultural essentialism and what the latter termed a 'nativist' approach, namely assuming that knowledge is inherently culturally bound and particularistic, and in the case of nativism, superior to other forms of knowledge.[24] At the heart of such an approach lies a replication of colonial invocations of intrinsic differences between the colonisers and the colonised. Just as we should be careful about assuming sameness (see above), we should be equally cautious about assuming and reifying difference. If we consider the example mentioned above about the experiences of people in

---

[24] For a discussion of the question of difference in the context of African thought, see Wiredu (1996), Hountondji (1997), Thiong'o (1986).

Southern Africa with borders, it is important to reiterate that these experiences are certainly not unique to the African continent. While there may be contextual nuances, there are also many similarities with the experiences of people living in border areas in other parts of the world: think for example of the fluidity of the borders in certain parts of Western Europe, and the ease with which people on both sides cross them.

Decentring

Decentring has become one of the more popular approaches to thinking globally about world politics. As with 'non-Western IR', the label itself promises a lot. Indeed, many scholars who take up decentring as their research strategy consider themselves following in the footsteps of Dipesh Chakrabarty (2000), who made a case for "provincializing Europe" in his book of the same title. The terminology utilised by decentring IR approaches also have affinities with the Dependency School's (Cardoso & Faletto, 1979) centre-periphery theorising. Yet, there is no indication that decentring IR approaches understand centre and periphery as mutually constitutive (see, Bilgin, 2021a), hence our positioning of decentring somewhere toward the centre of our continuum.

Consider, for instance, Meghana Nayak and Eric Selbin's (2010) *Decentering International Relations*, where the authors sought to provincialise the body of knowledge produced in North America and Western Europe, highlighting that it is but one way of narrating the international, and showing that other ways are not only possible but that they presently exist. Insofar as IR knowledge has been produced in the US and Western Europe, Nayak and Selbin (2010: 4) wrote in their pioneering book, decentring is about "[challenging] the politics, concepts and practices that enable certain narratives of IR to be central". As another example, also consider Nora Fisher Onar and Kalypso Nicolaïdis' (2013) who called for decentring European Studies.[25] They described their task as one of countering Eurocentrism in European Studies, which they understood as a narrative that the European Union tells itself through papering over the colonial past of its members. Onar and Nicolaïdis' approach to decentring, then, was about revealing the ways in which European great powers'

---

[25] Building on these attempts to decentre Europe, also see Keukeleire and Lecocq (2018), discussed in Chapter 5.

colonialism has been constitutive of 'Europe'. As a strategy for decentring, they suggested that scholars seek to "engage" and "learn from the other". How to do this? They wrote: "one can seek out other accounts of the world, and one can unpack those accounts to better understand the worldviews and value systems by which they are underpinned" (Onar & Nicolaïdis, 2013: 289).

Of these two efforts, Nayak and Selbin come closest to pursuing Chakrabarty's agenda for decentring 'Europe'. In his study, Chakrabarty had put Europe in its place as another geographical location, while insisting that the Europe that he seeks to provincialise is an "imaginary entity" that was spread throughout the globe through imperialism and Third World nationalism (2000: 42–3). Accordingly, decentring Europe, for Chakrabarty, was about "exploring how this thought—which is not everybody's heritage and which affects us all—may be renewed from and for the margins". Seen in this light, Chakrabarty did not come across as envisioning decentring solely by way of looking outside 'Europe', as with Onar and Nicolaïdis.

What is common to both Nayak and Selbin, and Onar and Nicolaïdis' decentring IR efforts is the way in which they portrayed those outside the 'centre' as if they are new entrants to the international, thereby overlooking their past constitutive relationship with the 'centre', albeit unintendedly. To clarify, on the one hand, decentring approaches do acknowledge the material exploitation and identity construction dynamics between centre and periphery when they highlight the ways in which the periphery has provided bodies and lands whose labour and riches were usurped by the centre or served an/the 'other' to centre's 'self'. Yet, on the other hand, they fail to consider those outside the centre as thinking actors who have been co-constitutive of those ideas, practices and institutions that are otherwise portrayed as having autonomously developed by the centre. Put differently, in decentring IR approaches, those outside the centre make an appearance as having been deprived of their material riches, or as the/an 'other' to the centre's 'self' (Bilgin, 2021a). What is missing is an understanding of the periphery as fellow (read: coeval) thinkers who have been a part of what Sankaran Krishna (1993: 388) referred to as "the intimate dialogue between 'Western' and 'non-Western' economies, societies, and philosophies". The different experiences of those at the 'centre' and those outside did not come about autonomously but in relationship to each other. What is more, such relations were not isolated to the extraction of material resources and/or self/other dynamics, but also comprised learning.

To recap, the four approaches that we have considered thus far each presumes a different origin for ideas while allowing for communication after-the-fact. As such, they offer us limited help in capturing the beginnings of ideas and knowledge about how the world works. To be able to explore beginnings, we turn to the following four approaches, which are located on the latter half of our continuum.

Historical Connections

We begin with a group of approaches that explicitly focus on connections, historically conceived. This entails investigating what Lewis Gordon (2019: 79) referred to as "the ongoing presence of the non-Western in the very advancement of the Western" whilst recognizing that "the 'outsider' is, after all, paradoxically also an 'insider'. We know, for example, that it is impossible to understand the development of modern art in Western Europe and North America without taking into account the influence of Japanese and African art on artists such as Vincent Van Gogh and Pablo Picasso. Similarly, scientific discoveries and progress are equally the result of exchanges of ideas across space and time.[26]

In response to the prevalent marginalisation of Africa's role in the shaping of global order, Howard French (2021) set out to centre Africa and Africans in the making of the modern world, challenging a deterministic account of Western ascendancy based on science and reason. In illuminating the "deeply twinned and tragic history of Africa and Europe" French (2021: 3) reimagined African agency by building on existing historical work that shows how the rise of Western Europe—associated with increased prosperity and scientific advances based on innate superiority—is inextricably linked to its encounters with Africa.

In IR, examples of scholars who have done this kind of work include John Hobson (2004), and Barry Buzan and George Lawson (2015). In his studies, Hobson showed how the emphasis on Westphalian understandings of sovereignty in IR overlooks the role of the East as being co-constitutive in the development of sovereignty (2009), and explored

---

[26] See, for example, James Poskett's book *Horizons* (2022), in which he argues that what is claimed to be 'Western' science is the result of global cultural exchanges.

what he referred to as 'the Eastern origins of the Western civilisation' (2004) and the 'multicultural origins of the global economy' (2020). In *The Global Transformation,* Buzan and Lawson (2015) offered what they termed a 'composite approach' to studying international history that understands modernity not in terms of factors endogenous to 'Europe' but as a product of 'uneven and combined' international relations of the long nineteenth century.

Phrased in Saidian terms, studying historical connections as such is one way of questioning the idea that modernity, or other developments typically associated with 'Europe' were in fact not purely from 'Europe' in origin, but that they are the results of historical relations of give-and-take between actors. While scholars have used different methods in doing this work, it has mainly entailed historical, archival work in order to trace the development of institutions and practices.

That said, some critics view the approach of emphasising historical connections as a valuable yet limited endeavour. Sanjay Seth (2009: 335–336), for example, noted that these battles are conducted "largely on the terrain of the empirical", which, in turn, has meant that "problems of the politics of knowledge remain, precisely because the central categories of the social sciences are the product of a European history". Seth's preferred approach contests the very concepts through which dominant accounts are told. In other words,

> it may not just be the 'content' of the social sciences (the explanations they offer, the narratives they construct) that is shaped by a genealogy that is both European and colonial, but their very 'form' (the concepts through which explanations become possible, including the very idea of what counts as an explanation). (Seth, 2009: 336)

Put differently, studies exploring historical connections seek to address the normative and/or analytical dimensions of Eurocentrism, while leaving the epistemological dimension largely untouched.[27] That being said, Seth insisted that these approaches are not mutually contradictory and can therefore be complementary.

A related critique was advanced by Zeynep Gülşah Çapan (2020), who argued that teasing out the role of historical connections in the production of knowledge does not sufficiently problematise the spatio-temporal

---

[27] For a discussion on Eurocentrism, see Chapter 1.

hierarchies that sustain a particular narrative of the international. This is because, while the role of 'non-Europe' is recognized and "brought in", it is still brought in on the terms of 'Europe'. It includes the notion that only knowledge that is viewed as legitimate is considered (for example, written archives outside North America and Western Europe). As with Seth, then, she too found the literature on historical connections wanting in addressing the epistemological dimension of Eurocentrism. Çapan (2020: 290) argued instead that the way to overcome this is to write "*coeval* and *co-present* histories of the international [original emphasis]".

To conclude, when the 'thing' that we study is not only material goods or institutions of world politics but ideas and knowledge regarding how the world works (as is our focus in this book), we need to go beyond understanding the history of the world as a relay race in which the baton of 'civilisation' is passed on to the next runner (as sometimes implicit in the scholarship on historical connections) but an exercise in studying "beginnings" (Said, 1975). This entails paying attention to what others have thought about the world and how it works.

Relationality

The study of relationality has a long history in IR (see, for example, Kurki, 2022; Kavalski, 2023) and over the years, a variety of IR theories and approaches have engaged with relational thinking, albeit in very different ways (Nordin et al., 2019). Milja Kurki (2022: 828) regards the differences and disagreements between relational approaches as a strength, noting that

> the relational turn is...quite distinct in arguing for *multiple* relational ways of understanding the world and arguably new kinds of debate around how we can place in conversations with each other relational perspectives of varied kind, from varied parts of the world (without assuming the superiority of specific relational ontologies.

Some have divided relational thinking according to their Anglophone of Sinophone origins (Qin & Nordin, 2019) although there has also been increased recognition of the relational underpinnings of much Indigenous thought in different parts of the world (Trownsell et al., 2022). In recent years, relational approaches have come to the fore insofar as they have been seen as promising to overcome IR's Eurocentrism. Here we will explicitly focus on those scholars who have self-consciously engaged in relational theorising with the aim of addressing Eurocentrism in IR.[28]

Notwithstanding their differences, relational approaches have in common a focus on ontology (challenging the substantialism associated with conventional IR),[29] and to a certain extent on epistemology as warranted by multiple ontological registers. We have placed relationality here towards the far end of the continuum, because its underlying premise suggests that relations exist prior to actors and that all actors are intimately connected. In this way, relational approaches privilege interconnectedness as an ontological starting point, and hold that actors, their identities and interests are shaped through constant processes of interaction. There is also an emphasis on the coexistence of and entwinement between a diversity of worldviews. Rather than viewing them as separate, a relational approach encourages us to consider their entanglement.

That said, despite relationality's promise to think beyond binaries and pre-given differences, some of this work can be seen as replicating some of the challenges posed by 'worlding as (geocultural) situatedness', insofar as the contributors to this literature presume fundamental ontological differences between 'Europe' and the rest of the world. Consider for instance the assumption that in certain parts of the world relational thinking is part of the culture in a way that it is not in other parts of the world. While the goal "to engage more effectively with others who start with other existential premises in order to have a better chance at synergistically diversifying our existential toolbox for the welfare of all life on the planet" (Trownsell, 2021: 803 f812) is a commendable one, there is also the danger of (over-) emphasising if not reifying difference, with all of the pitfalls this entails.

Consider also Qin's (2018) Confucian-inspired *Relational Theory of World Politics*, which is perhaps the most well-known explication of a relational approach to IR. In this book, Qin argued that culture matters in the construction of theory because the theoretical core is primarily shaped by the background knowledge of a cultural community. Contrasting Chinese with European culture, he contends that the latter is based on an individualist ontology, whereas the former subscribes to a relational ontology.

---

[28] See recent fora and special issues on relationality: Behera et al. (2022), Trownsell et al. (2021), Nordin et al. (2019).

[29] In simple terms, substantialism is the assumption that the entities studied in world politics (such as states) exist prior to interaction.

This, according to him, has important implications for IR, including that, from a relational perspective, the international system should be understood as a universe of interrelatedness rather than discrete entities, and that actors can only be actors-in-relations and therefore do not have predetermined identities, properties or interests. Qin and other scholars have drawn on relational thinking to make sense of China's foreign policy behaviour,[30] for instance, providing alternative explanations to those from conventional accounts such as neo-realism. However, in focusing on how China is different based on its unique culture and history and claiming that alternative theories are therefore required to make sense of it, the significance of connections and the way in which China has been worlded in terms of its identity and interests are overlooked.

As such, the way Qin has utilised relationality could be seen as belonging on the first half of our continuum, where ideas are presumed to originate in one place and then enter into relations with others. This has led some critics (for example, Shih, 2022) to argue that instead of transcending the binaries associated with substantialism in IR, some scholars have reproduced them instead. That said, there are relational approaches that consciously try to overcome presumptions of primordial difference by focusing on the mutual embeddedness and co-constitution of self and other.[31] As one example of such an approach, we turn to Ling's worldism.[32]

Worldism

Worldism is an approach to thinking globally about world politics developed by L. H. M. Ling throughout the 2000s in her single-authored and collaborative works (Agathangelou & Ling, 2009; Ling, 2013, 2014). While worldism understands world politics as being "a site of multiple worlds" (Agathangelou & Ling, 2009: 85) the emphasis is not only on the difference between these worlds but also on their entanglements and entwinements. Through various forms of engagements

---

[30] See for example Shih et al. (2019).

[31] This distinction is important as, according to a relational understanding of the world, the focus should not be on relations between actors or entities (inter-action) but on relations as ontologically prior to actors. See Chapter 5 for an exploration with a focus on South African foreign policy.

[32] Others include: Fierke (2022), Shih (2016), Shimizu (2019).

(or "reverberations"), the self and other are mutually embedded, and the connections underlying apparent contradictions are emphasised by the authors. Ultimately, worldism is a "politics of multiple relations," assuming a relationality of multiple social ontologies, with relationality in this earlier interpretation understood as interaction (Agathangelou & Ling, 2009: 90–91)—later the emphasis would shift to co-constitution (see below).

More than a way of thinking differently about world politics, Ling offered worldism as an emancipatory project aimed at bringing about a less violent world. Whilst recognising worldism's intellectual indebtedness to constructivism, postmodernism, feminism, Marxism, and particularly postcolonialism (and simultaneously drawing on Buddhism, Confucianism and Daoism), Agathangelou and Ling (2009: 90) nevertheless contended that worldism allows us to go further in our analytical endeavours. While postcolonialism recognizes the existence of multiple worlds and that there is negotiation across them, it does not explain "*why* and *how*" this is done [original emphasis], they argued.[33] In contrast, they held, why and how are at the heart of worldism as a project, which "makes explicit the multiple worlds presumed by postcolonial theorising" (Agathangelou & Ling, 2009: 5).

In terms of research tools, worldism initially proposed a "relational-materialist methodology" (Agathangelou & Ling, 2009: 91). What is meant here was that in order to fully understand the social world, we need to see it as reflecting a dialectical relationship between relations and (materialist) structures. In her later work, Ling drew on Daoist dialectics as epistemology, replacing the relational materialism proposed by her and Agathangelou in their 2009 book. Challenging the methodological individualism that characterises conventional IR, Daoist dialectics "enables interaction across and within bordered ontologies like Self vs Other, West vs Rest, Westphalia World vs Multiple Worlds" (Ling, 2014: 38)[34] Methodological individualism, in turn, is based on a particular

---

[33] In a later elaboration on worldism, Ling provides a further criticism of postcolonialism's shortcomings, noting, "Postcolonial scholarship, however, remains captive to its own critique. Claims of alterity and difference notwithstanding, postcolonial scholarship rarely indicates what will take place after "decolonising," "decentring," and/or "provincializing" Westphalia World" (Ling, 2014: 34).

[34] There are of course exceptions: interpretive research methods generally follow a less prescriptive, linear approach.

understanding of the nature of science and, as relational theorists of the quantum variety tell us, a particular understanding of physics as Newtonian.[35] While methodological individualism essentially overlooks social relations, an approach based on relationality as envisaged by Ling does not centre individual actors but rather the relations between them. In her choice of Daoist dialectics as a methodology, Ling made the point that it differs from the more well-known dialectical tradition in the social sciences based on the work of Hegel and Marx (Ling, 2014: 40). In other words, yin and yang, as opposites, are not entirely separate or different as they have within them pockets of co-implication. This also allowed Ling to address limitations of some postcolonial approaches. She contended that "we must be wary of theorising as the "Other" only. That is, we must accept that (1) Westphalia World is inside us as much as we are inside Westphalia World; consequently, (2) we must query our own assumptions, especially regarding the embodiments of world politics through race, gender, and class, and (3) examine how these intersect with the Westphalian state" (Ling, 2014: 34). Rephrased in the language used in Chapter 2, then, Ling suggested that 'worlding as (geocultural) situatedness' is not enough by itself unless we also analyse how IR and ir has worlded us (worlding as constitutive). She wrote:

> Worldism does not seek only to show how marginalised or erased actors affect world politics through civilizational processes or dialogics. Worldism extends upon this premise to highlight their *actual* ontological parity with, and thereby potential to balance, Westphalia World. At the same time, worldism takes Westphalia World to task for denying this history of abusive intimacy. Redressing this omission, however, does not mean replacing, abandoning, or 'forget[ting] IR.' Rather, worldism works with, through, and beyond Westphalia World. Worldism's model of dialogics specifies creative speaking and listening *among* Multiple Worlds as well as with Westphalia World. Only in this way could we re-balance and re-center world politics. (Ling, 2014: 2)

Indeed, Ling was at pains to emphasise that worldism is not only a more pluralist or cosmopolitan version of Westphalianism. In an implicit critique of 'geocultural pluralism' and 'non-Western IR' (see above), Ling (2014: 27) wrote:

---

[35] For an exploration of Quantum physics and Asian philosophies and a discussion on its implications for IR, see Fierke (2022).

That is, we study a cut of Confucianism here, a string of Hinduism there, like gems under glass in a museum, each isolated from the other as well as divorced from our 'modern' lives yet still functioning, somehow, in a Westphalian inter-state system of self-enclosed, competitive national units. Rather, worldism investigates the linkages among and within articulations of difference, and how these co-create an entwined complex of relations, socially *and* structurally, epistemically *and* normatively, to amount to what we call world politics....In this sense, worldism recognizes but does not restrict itself to "national schools of IR," like those from China, Japan, or India, nor does it attempt to resurrect area studies in IR.

In an interconnected world, to what extent can any knowledge claim to be purely autochthonous? Daoist dialectics suggests that the answer doesn't have to be either/or, as it allows for complementarities to prevail despite the contradictions between and within the polarities. In yin and yang, because each retains elements of the other within, all social identities are recognized as forever entwined, reinforcing the Daoist notion that despite differences, there are also similarities. Underlying this is a deeply relational understanding of the world.

Contrapuntal Reading and the Study of 'Constitutive Outside'

Contrapuntal reading is the method (author's choice of term) Said developed in *Culture and Imperialism* (1993). Here, he explored how the exile's "plurality of vision" could be turned into a method to study the impact of imperialism on the world. Himself a former subject of the British Empire, Said reflected on his own experiences when he noted that

> Many of us who grew up in the colonial era were struck by the fact that even though a hard and fast line separated coloniser from colonised in matters of rule and authority (a native could never aspire to the condition of the white man), the experiences of ruler and ruled were not so easily disentangled. On both sides of the imperial divide men and women shared experiences—though differently inflected experiences-through education, civic life, memory, war (Said, 2003: para. 7).

It is to be able to study such connections and get away from the objective/subjective dichotomy that Fanon found exasperating (see above), argued Said, that we need a new method. The idea, according to him (Said, 2000b: 99), was "to read texts from the metropolitan centre and from the peripheries contrapuntally, neither according the privilege of 'objectivity' to our side nor the encumbrance of 'subjectivity' to theirs."

As such, Said's method of 'contrapuntal reading' is not to be confused with the 'voyage in'. Instead, the 'voyage in' is:

> the work of intellectuals from the colonial or peripheral regions of the world, intellectuals who wrote not in a native language but in an 'imperial' language, who felt themselves to be organically tied to a mass effort at resisting imperial rule, and who set themselves the specifically revisionist and critical task of dealing frontally with the hegemonic culture in new, radically provocative ways. (Said, 2000b: 81)

Accordingly, 'the voyage in' produces "a specially interesting variety of hybrid cultural work" (Said, 2003: 82–83) which could, then, be utilised for the purposes of contrapuntal reading. Indeed, this is what Said delivered in *Culture and Imperialism*, reading the products of, say, the Subaltern Studies group (which he considers as examples of 'the voyage in') contrapuntally with those of the imperial metropole. Here is how Said (2000b: 100) elaborated on his method:

> [I]t is a radical falsification of culture to strip it of its affiliations with its setting, or to pry it away from the terrain it contested. Jane Austen's Mansfield Park is about England and about Antigua, and the connection is made explicitly by Austen; it is therefore about order at home and slavery abroad, and can - indeed ought - to be read that way, with Williams and James alongside the book. Similarly Camus and Gide write about precisely the same Algeria written about by Fanon and Kateb Yacine.

What does Said's method of contrapuntal reading offer for IR? Remember that we placed the approaches we have discussed in this chapter on our continuum based on the degree to which they capture multiple beginnings of ideas and knowledge about how the world works. Contrapuntal reading is placed at the latter part of the continuum insofar as it is designed to study connections beyond those explored by above-mentioned approaches. More precisely, contrapuntal reading helps us to study the ways in which those other parts of the world are the 'constitutive outside' to 'Europe'—not only in material or institutional terms (as explored by historical connections literature) but also ideational terms.[36] The notion of 'constitutive outside'[37] was elaborated on by cultural theorist Stuart Hall (1996: 249) in his discussion on how "the whole process of expansion, exploration, conquest, colonisation and imperial hegemonisation... [has] constituted the 'outer face', the constitutive outside, of European and then Western capitalist modernity after 1492." Most importantly for the purposes of this book, this is true not only for material contributions as explored by the literature on historical connections (see above), but also for ideas and knowledge (Bhambra, 2007; Bhambra & Shilliam, 2009; Grovogui, 2006).

The fact that the insights and experiences of the world outside 'Europe' are not reflected in conventional or critical IR narratives does not mean that they were literally absent. It only means that their insights, interventions, experiences and inputs are not included in those particular narratives. Put differently, those from 'non-Europe' are outside by virtue of having been left out of those narratives that we get to hear about the international. They are also constitutive because those ideas, practices, and institutions that are typically ascribed to 'Europe' have been co-constituted together with other parts of the world.[38]

As heuristics, we identify three dynamics to Europe's constitutive outside. These are, material exploitative, self/other and ideational. While the first and/or second of these three dimensions are appreciated by scholars seeking to decentre IR and those who explore historical connections, the third is rendered invisible. The rest of the world has been constitutive of 'Europe' not only by providing bodies and lands whose labour and riches were exploited, and other/s as foil to one's self, but also as thinking actors who have produced ideas of their own and together with others.

Since our focus in Chapter 3 is on ideas and knowledge about how the world works, let us pick our illustrations from IR theory. As post-colonial voices began to get themselves heard in a variety of fields,

---

[36] Also see Chapter 4.

[37] The concept is also utilised in Post-structuralist Political thought and History, albeit in different ways.

[38] Let us also note that this is not the same point that R. B. J. Walker (2006) made when he discussed the 'double outsides' of the international.

criticisms regarding their indebtedness to post-structuralist thought began to surface (see, for example, Acharya & Buzan, 2007: 308; cf. Ahluwalia, 2005). The charge raised against postcolonial IR was two-fold: that post-colonial thought is not original but derivative; and that postcolonialism has remained remote from the concerns of the formerly colonised. Yet, when someone questions the relevance of postcolonial critique in the study of Africa by virtue of its indebtedness to, say, Pierre Bourdieu, the appropriate response is not only to ponder 'how theories travel', but also to highlight the ways in which Bourdieu's work is already informed by his experiences in Algeria and his collaboration with "Algerian sociologist Abdelmayek Sayad who believed that immigration and citizenship policies revealed what states thought of themselves' (Guiraudon, 2012: 207). To re-state what is at stake in inquiring into post-colonial critique as post-structuralist thought's 'constitutive outside": revealing post-structuralist thought's blindness to the constitutive role played by the colonial context; highlighting post-structuralist thought's failure to remedy its blindness notwithstanding critical voices who pointed to the constitutive role of colonialism; and pointing to post-structuralist thought's failure to reflect on the post-colonial critique as its 'constitutive outside'.

Conclusion

While this chapter discussed approaches available to us as students when seeking to think globally about world politics, it is important to empha-sise again that there is not one definitive solution. It is also in the nature of thinking globally about world politics to allow for a multiplicity of approaches. While we have made clear which approaches we think are not counterproductive given the task of thinking globally about world politics, ultimately the decision is left to the researcher depending on what they are puzzled by. As such, thinking globally about world politics entails letting go of a sense of certainty about what we know about the world, to being genuinely puzzled, and to being comfortable with a degree of discomfort inherent in 'exile as metaphor'. It is this living with a degree of discom-fort that scholars who have been doing this work (see the Postscript) emphasise as essential to thinking globally about world politics.

Bibliography

Abraham, I. (1998). *The Making of the Indian Atomic Bomb: Science, Secrecy and the Postcolonial State*. Zed Books.

Abraham, I. (2006). The Contradictory Spaces of Postcolonial Techno-Science. *Economic and Political Weekly*, 210–217.

Acharya, A. (2014). Global International Relations (IR) and Regional Worlds. *International Studies Quarterly, 58*(4), 647–659.

Acharya, A., & Buzan, B. (2007). Why is There no Non-Western International Relations Theory? An Introduction. *International Relations of the Asia-Pacific, 7*(3), 287–312.

Ackerly, B., & True, J. (2010). *Back to the Future: Feminist Theory, Activism, and Doing Feminist Research in an Age of Globalization*. Paper presented at the Women's Studies International Forum.

Agathangelou, A. M. (2016). Archives are Part of International Knowledge, Not Merely Happenstance: In Conversation with Siba Grovogui. *Comparative Studies of South Asia, Africa and the Middle East, 36*(1), 204–212.

Agathangelou, A. M., & Ling, L. H. M. (2009). *Transforming World Politics: From Empire to Multiple Worlds*. Taylor and Francis.

Ahluwalia, P. (2005). Out of Africa: Post-structuralism's Colonial Roots. *Postcolonial Studies, 8*(2), 137–154.

Alker, H. R. (1996). *Rediscoveries and Reformulations: Humanistic Methodologies for International Studies*. Cambridge University Press.

Behera, N. C., Shani, G., & Trownsell, T. (2022). Introduction to the Special Issue: Pluriversal relationality. *Review of International Studies, 48*(5), 787–800.

Beier, J. M. (2005). *International Relations in Uncommon Places: Indigeneity, Cosmology, and the Limits of International Theory*. Palgrave Macmillan.

Bhambra, G. K. (2007). *Rethinking Modernity: Postcolonialism and the Sociological Imagination*. Palgrave.

Bhambra, G. K., & Shilliam, R. (2009). *Silencing Human Rights: Critical Engagements with a Contested Project*. Palgrave Macmillan.

Bilgin, P. (2008). Thinking Past 'Western' IR? *Third World Quarterly, 29*(1), 5–23.

Bilgin, P. (2012). Security in the Arab World and Turkey: Differently Different. In A. Tickner & D. Blaney (Eds.), *Thinking International Relations Differently* (Vol. 2, pp. 27–47). Routledge.

Bilgin, P. (2016). *The International in Security, Security in the International*. Routledge.

Bilgin, P. (2021a). How Not to Globalise IR: 'Centre'and 'Periphery' as Constitutive of 'the International.' *Uluslararası İlişkiler Dergisi, 18*(70), 13–27.

Bilgin, P. (2021b). On the 'Does Theory Travel?' Question: Traveling with Edward Said. In Z. G. Capan, F. Dos Reis, & M. Grasten (Eds.), *The Politics of Translation in International Relations* (pp. 245–255). Springer.

Bilgin, P., & Çapan, Z. G. (2021). Introduction to the Special Issue Regional International Relations and Global Worlds: Globalising International Relations. *Uluslararası İlişkiler Dergisi*, 18(70), 1–11.

Björkdahl, A., Hall, M., & Svensson, T. (2019). Everyday International Relations: Editors' Introduction. *Cooperation and Conflict*, 54(2), 123–130.

Blaney, D. L., & Inayatullah, N. (2008). International Relations from Below. In C. Reus-Smit & D. Snidal (Eds.), *The Oxford Handbook of International Relations* (pp. 663–674). Oxford University Press.

Bleiker, R. (2017). In Search of Thinking Space: Reflections on the Aesthetic Turn in International Political Theory. *Millennium: Journal of International Studies*, 45(2), 258–264.

Bleiker, R. (2018). Mapping Visual Global Politics. In R. Bleiker (Ed.), *Visual Global Politics* (pp. 1–30). Routledge.

Boatcă, M. (2015). The Quasi-Europes: World Regions in Light of the Imperial Difference. In T. Reifer (Ed.), *Global Crises and the Challenges of the 21st Century* (pp. 132–153). Routledge.

Buzan, B., & Lawson, G. (2015). *The Global Transformation: History, Modernity and the Making of International Relations*. Cambridge University Press.

Capan, Z. G. (2020). Beyond Visible Entanglements: Connected Histories of the International. *International Studies Review*, 22(2), 289–306.

Cardoso, F. H., & Faletto, E. (1979). *Dependency and Development in Latin America*. University of California Press.

Chakrabarty, D. (2000). *Provincializing Europe: Postcolonial Thought and Historical Difference*. Princeton University Press.

Chan, G. (1999). Towards an IR Theory with Chinese Characteristics. In G. Chan (Ed.), *Chinese Perspectives on International Relations: A Framework for Analysis* (pp. 139–161). Palgrave Macmillan UK.

Chan, S. (2017). *Plural International Relations in a Divided World*. John Wiley and Sons.

Chen, C.-C. (2012). The Im/possibility of Building Indigenous Theories in a Hegemonic Discipline: The Case of Japanese International Relations. *Asian Perspective*, 36(3), 463–492.

Chen, C. C., & Shimizu, K. (2019). International relations from the margins: the Westphalian meta-narratives and counter-narratives in Okinawa–Taiwan relations. *Cambridge Review of International Affairs*, 32(4), 521–540.

Darby, P. (2006). *Postcolonizing the International: Working to Change the Way We are*. University of Hawaii Press.

Davis, A. E., Thakur, V., & Vale, P. (2020). *The Imperial Discipline*. Pluto.

de Koeijer, V., & Shilliam, R. (2021). Forum: International Relations as a Geoculturally Pluralistic Field. *International Politics Reviews, 9*(2), 272–275.

Drulák, P. (2009). Special Forum Section: International Relations (IR) in Central and Eastern Europe *Journal of International Relations and Development, 12*(2), 168–173.

Dussel, E. (1993). Eurocentrism and Modernity (Introduction to the Frankfurt Lectures). *Boundary 2, 20*(3), 65–76.

El-Malik, S. S., & Kamola, I. A. (Eds.). (2017). *Politics of African Anticolonial Archive*. Rowman and Littlefield.

Enloe, C. (2011). The Mundane Matters. *International Political Sociology, 5*(4), 447–450.

Fierke, K. M. (2022). *Snapshots from Home: Mind, Action and Strategy in an Uncertain World*. Bristol University Press.

French, H. W. (2021). *Born in Blackness: Africa, Africans, and the Making of the Modern World, 1471 to the Second World War*. Liveright Publishing.

Gallagher, J. (2022). *Introduction: Understanding Statehood Through Architecture*. https://www.africanstatearchitecture.co.uk/

Gordon, L. R. (2019). Problematic People and Epistemic Decolonization: Toward the Postcolonial in Africana Political Thought. In *Knowledges Born in the Struggle* (pp. 78–95). Routledge.

Grovogui, S. N. (2006). *Beyond Eurocentrism and Anarchy: Memories of International Order and Institutions*. Palgrave Macmillan.

Grovogui, S. N. (2023). Putin's Ukraine Aggression: How Should an African Respond? *International Politics, 60*, 214–235.

Guiraudon, V. (2012). Citizenship: Bourdieu, Migration and the International. In R. Adler-Nissen (Ed.), *Bourdieu in International Relations: Rethinking Key Concepts in IR* (pp. 207–219). Routledge.

Hall, S. (1996). When was 'The Post-colonial'? Thinking at the Limit. In I. Chambers & L. Curti (Eds.), *The Post-colonial Question: Common Skies, Divided Horizons* (pp. 242–262). Routledge.

Harding, S. G. (1987). *Feminism and Methodology: Social Science Issues*. Indiana University Press.

Harding, S. G. (1991). *Whose Science? Whose Knowledge? Thinking from Women's Lives*. Cornell University Press.

Harding, S. G. (Ed.). (2004). *The Feminist Standpoint Theory Reader: Intellectual and Political Controversies*. Routledge.

Harman, S. (2019). *Seeing Politics: Film, Visual Method, and International Relations*. McGill-Queen's Press-MQUP.

Hazbun, W. (2016). Assembling Security in a 'Weak State': The Contentious Politics of Plural Governance in Lebanon Since 2005. *Third World Quarterly, 37*(6), 1053–1070.

Hobson, J. M. (2004). *The Eastern Origins of Western Civilization*. Cambridge University Press.

Hobson, J. M. (2009). Provincializing Westphalia: The Eastern Origins of Sovereignty. *International Politics, 46*, 671–690.

Hobson, J. M. (2020). *Multicultural Origins of the Global Economy': Beyond the Western-Centric Frontier*. Cambridge University Press.

Hountondji, P. J. (Ed.) (1997). *Endogenous Knowledge: Research Trails*. CODESRIA.

Kavalski, E. (2023). Relational Theories in International Relations. In *Oxford Research Encyclopedia of International Studies*.

Keukeleire, S., & Lecocq, S. (2018). Operationalising the Decentring Agenda: Analysing European Foreign Policy in a non-European and Post-Western World. *Cooperation and Conflict, 53*(2), 277–295.

Krishna, S. (1993). The Importance of Being Ironic: A Postcolonial View on Critical International Relations Theory. *Alternatives, 18*(3), 385–417.

Kurki, M. (2022). Relational Revolution and Relationality in IR: New Conversations. *Review of International Studies, 48*(5), 821–836.

Levine, D. J., & McCourt, D. M. (2018). Why Does Pluralism Matter When We Study Politics? A View from Contemporary International Relations. *Perspectives on Politics, 16*(1), 92–109.

Ling, L. H. M. (2013). Worlds Beyond Westphalia: Daoist Dialectics and the 'China Threat.' *Review of International Studies, 39*(3), 549–568.

Ling, L. H. M. (2014). *The Dao of World Politics: Towards a Post-Westphalian, Worldist International Relations*. Routledge.

Lorde, A. (2012 (1984)). *Sister Outsider: Essays and Speeches*. Crossing Press.

Mayblin, L. (n.d.). *Border Thinking*, https://globalsocialtheory.org/concepts/border-thinking/

Mbembe, A. (2002). African Modes of Self-Writing. *Public Culture, 14*(1), 239–273.

McGrane, B. (1989). *Beyond Anthropology: Society and the Other*. Columbia University Press.

Mignolo, W. (2013). Geopolitics of Sensing and Knowing: On (de) coloniality, Border Thinking, and Epistemic Disobedience. *Confero: Essays on Education, Philosophy and Politics, 1*(1), 129–150.

Mitchell, T. (1989). The World as Exhibition. *Comparative Studies in Society and History, 31*(2), 217–236.

Möller, F., & Shim, D. (2019). Visions of Peace in International Relations. *International Studies Perspectives, 20*(3), 246–264.

Morefield, J. (2022). *Unsettling the World: Edward Said and Political Theory*. Rowman and Littlefield.

Narayan, U. (1998). Essence of Culture and a Sense of History: A Feminist Critique of Cultural Essentialism. *Hypatia, 13*(2), 86–106.

Narayan, U. (2004). The Project of Feminist Epistemology: Perspectives of a NonWestern Feminist. In S. Harding (Ed.), *The Feminist Standpoint Theory Reader: Intellectual and Political Controversies* (pp. 213–224). Routledge.

Nayak, M., & Selbin, E. (2010). *Decentering International Relations*. Zed Books.

Nordin, A. H. M., Smith, G. M., Bunskoek, R., Huang, C. C., Hwang, Y. J., Jackson, P. T., & Zalewski, M. (2019). Towards Global Relational Theorizing: A Dialogue Between Sinophone and Anglophone Scholarship on Relationalism. *Cambridge Review of International Affairs, 32*(5), 570–581.

Onar, N. F., & Nicolaïdis, K. (2013). The Decentring Agenda: Europe as a Post-colonial Power. *Cooperation and Conflict, 48*(2), 283–303.

Poskett, J. (2022). *Horizons: A Global History of Science*. Penguin UK.

Qin, Y. (2013). An Accidental (Chinese) International Relations Theorist. In A. B. Tickner & D. Blaney (Eds.), *Claiming the International*. Routledge.

Qin, Y. (2018). *A Relational Theory of World Politics*. Cambridge University Press.

Qin, Y., & Nordin, A. H. (2019). Relationality and Rationality in Confucian and Western Traditions of Thought. *Cambridge Review of International Affairs, 32*(5), 601–614.

Said, E. W. (1975). *Beginnings: Intention and Method*. Basic Books.

Said, E. W. (1978). *Orientalism*. Penguin.

Said, E. W. (1984). Reflections on Exile. *Granta, 13*(Autumn), 157–172.

Said, E. W. (1993). *Culture and Imperialism*. Knopf.

Said, E. W. (1999). *Out of Place: A Memoir* (1st ed.). Knopf.

Said, E. W. (2000a). *Reflections on Exile and Other Essays*. Harvard University Press.

Said, E. W. (2000b). The Voyage In: Third World Intellectuals and Metropolitan Cultures. In D. Hopwood (Ed.), *Arab Nation, Arab Nationalism* (pp. 79–101). Palgrave Macmillan UK.

Said, E. W. (2003). Always on Top. *London Review of Books, 25*(6).

Seo, J., & Cho, Y. C. (2021). The Emergence and Evolution of International Relations Studies in Postcolonial South Korea. *Review of International Studies, 47*(5), 619–636.

Seth, S. (2009). Historical Sociology and Postcolonial Theory: Two Strategies for Challenging Eurocentrism. *International Political Sociology, 3*(3), 334–338.

Shani, G. (2008). Toward a Post-Western IR: The Umma, Khalsa Panth, and Critical International Relations Theory. *International Studies Review, 10*(4), 722–734.

Shih, C., Huang, C., Yeophantong, P., Bunskoek, R.,, Ikeda, J., Hwang, J., Wang, H., Chang, C., & Chen, C. (2019). *China and International Theory: The Balance of Relationships*. Routledge.

Shih, C.-Y. (2022). *Post-Chineseness: Cultural Politics and International Relations*. State University of New York Press.

Shih, C.-Y. (2016). Affirmative Balance of the Singapore–Taiwan Relationship: A Bilateral Perspective on the Relational Turn in International Relations. *International Studies Review, 18*(4), 681–701.

Shilliam, R. (2014). "Open the Gates Mek We Repatriate": Caribbean Slavery, Constructivism, and Hermeneutic Tensions. *International Theory, 6,* 349–372.

Shilliam, R. (2021). *Decolonizing Politics: An Introduction.* Polity Press.

Sil, R., & Katzenstein, P. J. (2010). Analytic Eclecticism in the Study of World Politics: Reconfiguring Problems and Mechanisms Across Research Traditions. *Perspectives on Politics, 8*(2), 411–431.

Smith, K. (2021a). Challenging International Relations' Conceptual Constraints: The International and Everyday Life across Borders in Southern Africa. *Uluslararası İlişkiler Dergisi, 18*(70), 121–134.

Smith, L. T. (2021b). *Decolonizing Methodologies: Research and Indigenous Peoples.* Bloomsbury Publishing.

Thiong'o, N. W. (1986). *Decolonising the Mind: The Politics of Language in African Literature.* J. Currey.

Tickner, A. B., & Waever, O. (Eds.). (2009a). *International Relations Scholarship Around the World.* Routledge.

Tickner, A. B., & Waever, O. (2009b). Introduction: Geocultural epistemologies. In A. B. Tickner & O. Wæver (Eds.), *International Relations Scholarship Around the World.* Routledge.

Tickner, A. B., & Waever, O. (2009c). Conclusion: Worlding Where the West Once Was. In A. B. Tickner & O. Wæver (Eds.), *International Relations Scholarship Around the World.* Routledge.

Tieku, T. K. (2021). The Legon School of International Relations. *Review of International Studies, 47*(5), 656–671.

Trownsell, T. (2021). Recrafting Ontology. *Review of International Studies, 48*(5), 801–820.

Trownsell, T., Behera, N. C., & Shani, G. (2022). Introduction to the Special Issue: Pluriversal Relationality. *Review of International Studies, 48*(5), 787–800.

Trownsell, T. A., Tickner, A. B., Querejazu, A., Reddekop, J., Shani, G., Shimizu, K., Behera, N. C., & Arian, A. (2021). Differing about Difference: Relational IR from around the World. *International Studies Perspectives, 22*(1), 25–64.

Vázquez-Arroyo, A. Y. (2018). Critical Theory, Colonialism, and the Historicity of Thought. *Constellations, 25*(1), 54–70.

Vitalis, R. (2018). *White World Order, Black Power Politics: The Birth of American International Relations.* Cornell University Press.

Vrasti, W. (2008). The Strange Case of Ethnography and International Relations. *Millennium: Journal of International Studies, 37*(2), 279–301.
Walker, R. B. J. (2006). The Double Outside of the Modern International. *Ephemera, 6*(1), 56–69.
Weber, C. (2015). Why is There no Queer International Theory? *European Journal of International Relations, 21*(1), 27–51.
Wiredu, K. (1996). *Cultural Universals and Particulars: An African Perspective.* Indiana University Press.

CHAPTER 4

Thinking Globally About (the Study of) Security

Pinar Bilgin

Abstract This chapter zooms in on one of the two main subfields of International Relations (IR), namely (International) Security Studies, to further highlight different ways of thinking globally about world politics. The chapter begins with the observation that international security has not always been studied in a manner true to its name. Second, lest it seems that Eurocentrism only limits the study of those parts of the world other than 'Europe', the chapter looks at the study of militarism, highlighting the ways in which the study of security in 'Europe' too has suffered. Next, the chapter turns to Critical Security Studies (CSS) and focuses on how CSS scholars have treated the Eurocentrism of ISS as an 'absence'. Finally, the chapter explores one way of thinking globally about security by utilising the notion of 'constitutive outside', so as to see how those who have been outside of our ISS narratives have been constitutive of security in theory and in practice.

Keywords Eurocentrism · The international · Critical security studies · Absence · Militarism · Nuclear weapons · Constitutive outside

P. Bilgin and K. Smith, *Thinking Globally About World Politics: Beyond Global IR*, https://doi.org/10.1007/978-3-031-56572-4_4

INTRODUCTION

Putting 'global' in front of security does not render its study global. The idea is not to replace 'international' with 'global' in name only, but to ask ourselves what thinking globally about (the study of) security entails. It means being curious about what others think about the world, making a sustained effort to locate what they have produced, and recognising past and present contributions to what we otherwise view as 'European' ideas, practices, and institutions. This chapter begins with the observation that international security has not always been studied in a manner true to its name. First, I locate the 'international' in the study of security, highlighting how International Security Studies (ISS) scholars privilege one dimension of 'security' (the military) and one way of thinking about the 'international' (anarchical). They do so by focusing on great powers' insecurities and by taking for granted their conception of the international. Second, lest it seems that Eurocentrism only limits the study of those parts of the world other than 'Europe',[1] I will look at the study of militarism, highlighting the ways in which the study of security in 'Europe' too has suffered. Next, I will turn to Critical Security Studies (CSS). Since the early 1990s, CSS scholars have sought to address the privileged place accorded to the military dimension of security. However, the privileged place accorded to the great powers' conception of the international has proven to be more persistent. I develop this point by considering how CSS scholars have treated the Eurocentrism of ISS as an 'absence'. Finally, I will explore one way of thinking globally about security. I will do this by utilising the notion of 'constitutive outside', so as to see how those who have been outside of our ISS narratives have been constitutive of security in theory and in practice.

LOCATING THE INTERNATIONAL IN INTERNATIONAL SECURITY (STUDIES)

Realists have approached international security in terms of the lack of what they think made domestic security possible: a (world) government. Their critics, even as they explored different ways of living in anarchy,

---

[1] In our use, 'Europe' refers to the birthplace of Eurocentrism, and includes both North America and Western Europe. See Chapter 1 for further discussion.

did not consider as relevant the possibility that conceiving of the international as anarchy was perhaps not (entirely) shared by others who also constitute the international (Bilgin, 2016). Here, it is important to disentangle the prevalent conception of the 'international as anarchy' from a less pronounced conception of the 'international as hierarchy'.[2] The latter was voiced by the so-called 'radicals' who pointed to economic structures at work in the shaping of world politics. Prominent examples include the Dependency School and the WorldSystems Theory scholars (Cardoso & Faletto, 1979; Wallerstein, 1974). Over the years, they were joined by feminist, postcolonial and decolonial approaches, who insisted that the hierarchical order of world politics was not only economic, but also gendered and racial with implications for the study of world politics.[3] Yet, during the Cold War, when great power insecurities were considered to be the most important by ISS scholars, the voices of the 'radicals' were marginalised.

That said, there was no glossing over the ways in which hierarches were embedded in international security. Consider Cold War protests against military bases around the world. The protesters were invariably silenced, but not because their agenda was not considered fitting within the military-focused frameworks of ISS. Women who lived next to military bases around the world (Enloe, 1990) or where nuclear weapons were situated in the United Kingdom (Sylvester, 1994) did focus on the military dimension of security. Yet, their security referent was different: human beings.

People versus states is not the only hierarchy; there is also a hierarchy between people of some states versus people of other states. Consider the following example: After the use of nuclear weapons against Japan by the United States in 1945, others also pursued their nuclear programs while the US sought to further develop its own. Developing nuclear weapons involves testing. After the early tests, which were conducted on the mainland, the US administration received advice to conduct nuclear

---

[2] While there have been attempts to render visible the 'hierarchy in anarchy' (Donnelly, 2006) or 'hierarchy under anarchy' (Wendt and Friedheim, 2009), their focus was on material and/or historical inequalities between states and/or institutionalised relationships of dependency. John Hobson and Jason Sharman (2005) and Robert Vitalis (2005) also highlighted the hierarchical element to anarchy, but not necessarily to find out about the perspectives of those lower down the hierarchy.

[3] See Chapter 2.

tests "overseas until it could be established more definitely that continental detonations would not endanger the public health and safety" (Mathur, 2020: 141). The Marshall Islands in the Pacific was one of the test sites. Responding to the critics, Henry Kissinger (1958) chided the protesters (as well as radical scholars and others who sought to amplify the concerns of the Marshall Islanders) for failing to appreciate what was important for maintaining international security at a time when the 'Free World' was under threat.[4] The implication of Kissinger's words being that people of some states were more dispensable than people of some other states.

The international as hierarchy was also problematised during the Cold War by the leaders of some African states. Joanne Sharp's (2013: 23) study of President Julius Nyerere highlighted how the Tanzanian leader viewed the international as "unaccountable to Africa and the South". Nyerere found such hierarchy to be less than democratic especially at a time when African leaders (such as himself) were coming under criticism for their less-than-democratic modes of governance (Chan, 2021). Nyerere's understanding of the international as hierarchy did not make it into the study of security at the time. But then, the hierarchy that President Nyerere challenged was not the same as the one revealed by Kissinger's response to the anti-nuclear protesters (i.e., people of some states versus people of other states). Nyerere highlighted a hierarchy between states: the great powers versus those in "Africa and the South".

So far, I have identified three cross-cutting hierarchies. These are: people versus states; people of some states versus people of other states; great powers versus other states. Whichever way you look at it, those people in "Africa and the South" (to use Nyerere's term) ended up on the "bottom rung" (Enloe, 1996) of hierarchies in world politics. As captured by Ritu Mathur (2020: 23), "differences in race, ethnicity, religion, class and 'lack of technological modernism' made the safety and security of subalterns a secondary consideration".

Abdel Monem Al-Mashat (1985), Bahgat Korany (1986), Mohamed Ayoob (1986, 1995), Edward Azar and Chung-in Moon (1988) and

---

[4] Kissinger was teaching at Harvard University at the time while serving in an advisory capacity for various public agencies and think tanks. From 1969 until 1977 Kissinger served in the US Government, first as National Security Advisor and later as Secretary of State.

Caroline Thomas, (1991) were singular in their interest in the insecurities in/of the Third World (scholars' choice of term). They studied the ways in which ISS concepts and theories focused on the insecurities of the great powers, and therefore were less than helpful in accounting for insecurities in/of the Third World. However, in doing so, they did not seek to rethink ISS concepts and theories with a view to making them more relevant everywhere. The upshot of which was that the international in security remained under-scrutinised, and the opportunity to inquire into the potential implications of their critique for the study of security writ large was squandered.

What if such an opportunity was not squandered? What would that look like? Let us consider the implications of the recent scholarship on race and IR for the study of security. We learn from revisionist accounts of the early years of IR that, at the turn of the twentieth century, those who were involved in (neo)colonialism were conscious of the international as hierarchy. While the colonised sought to alter their 'inferior' status, the (neo)colonisers sought to preserve their 'superiority'. A key event of the time was the Japanese Empire's victory against the Russian Empire in 1905, which had "presented white supremacy theory with a serious empirical problem" (Vitalis, 2005: 167–168). When those who were regarded as 'inferior' peoples not only fought back but also made advances, fears of a world-wide race war came to the fore. Such concerns did not disappear during the inter-war era but continued to shape post-WWII discussions on the coming world order, as captured in W. E. B. De Bois' (1946) *Color and Democracy*. The implication being that the study of IR (and security) was shaped by the great powers' understanding of the international, but not in the way told by well-known narratives on the UK and US origins of IR. It was not only great powers' concerns about another world war, but also about maintaining their (neo)colonial privileges in a potential world-wide race war that shaped the study of world politics at the time.[5]

To answer the 'what if' question from above, the implications of the recent scholarship on race and IR for the study of security is hard to miss. To those who were racialised, the international came across as hierarchical. But then, it was not only those who were racialised who conceived of the

---

[5] For example, the policy magazine *Foreign Affairs* was called the *Journal of Race Development* between 1910 and 1919.

international in this way. Insofar as the great powers sought to maintain their superior position vis-a-vis racialised others, the international as
hierarchy shaped their insecurities and their study of world politics. The
international as hierarchical was there, hidden in plain sight. That the
students of IR do not always know how their discipline was shaped by
the racial insecurities of the great powers of the early twentieth century
has to do with IR's Eurocentric limitations.[6] By maintaining the fiction
of the international as only anarchical, students of ISS remained oblivious
to the ways in which their concepts and theories were shaped as part of
an attempt to secure a hierarchical world order. Let me restate in practical terms: If, in present-day world politics, we are at a loss as to how to
make sense of not only different but also "differently different" (Bilgin,
2012a) thinking and other practices of state and non-state actors around
the world (including 'Europe', see below), this is because we have, for
a long time, failed to address our Eurocentric limitations. Our concepts
and theories are limited because they derive from a particular narrative (of
"what is said to have happened" in 'Europe', [Grovogui, 2006]) which,
in turn, has been challenged by revisionist accounts.

EUROCENTRISM IS A PROBLEM FOR THE STUDY
OF SECURITY IN 'EUROPE' TOO

Typically, students of ISS (or CSS, for that matter) are not overly
concerned with Eurocentrism if their studies focus on 'Europe' alone.
This is because the limitations of Eurocentrism are understood in terms
of ISS concepts and theories' ability to 'travel' to other parts of the
world,[7] the presumption being that they work just fine in 'Europe'. In
this section, I will look at the study of militarism in 'Europe' as a window
into the Eurocentric limitations of ISS, focusing on the ways in which (the
study of) insecurities experienced outside 'Europe' have had consequences
for (the study of) militarism inside.

Since the September 11, 2001 attacks, we have become increasingly
aware of the brute force and technology utilised by the police for purposes
of anti-terrorism and whatever else gets to be defined as 'terrorism' by
those authorities who find the label useful for governance purposes. This

---

[6] See Chapter 1.

[7] For a discussion on how theories 'travel', see Bilgin (2021).

eventuality was compounded in the US, among other places, by the furnishing of the police with the weapons that were brought back from the Gulf and Afghanistan (McCoy, 2016). Some have characterised this phenomenon as the 'militarisation of the police'. Others have objected, insisting that militarism is not new and that it has always been with us (Neocleous, 2013; also see, Mann, 1987).[8] Indeed, there is a rich feminist literature that has explored the militarisation of women's lives (Enloe, 1983, 1990). There is also a body of expertise on forms of militarism outside 'Europe' (Altınay, 2004; Ben-Eliezer, 1997; Diamint, 2015). That being said, while it is inaccurate to talk about this issue as if militarism did not exist before, following Julian Go (2024: 9) it needs acknowledging that there are "temporal rhythms, discontinuities and variations" as regards both its methods and targets.

Why, then, have we come to understand post-September 11 developments as militarisation, if militarism has always been with us in one form or another?[9] This is puzzling especially if we consider the wealth of research and expertise into militarism outside 'Europe' which partly overlaps with feminist research into militarism (inside *and* outside). Here is my answer: Because the international is missing in (the study of) militarism. I will build towards this answer by outlining the study of militarism in ISS and then consider an example.[10]

ISS definitions typically define militarism in terms of its most visible indicators, namely the glorification of military rule and or behaviour (see, Eastwood, 2018). Such behaviour, in turn, is found to exist in the past—be it 'Europe's past, as with Germany before and during World War II and Portugal, Spain and Greece before they transitioned to democracy in the 1970s, or our contemporaries elsewhere in the world who are viewed as belonging to a past world. As such, the world outside 'Europe' is portrayed as an anachronism by virtue of its failure to leave behind

---

[8] Here, it is important to note that the inside/outside division of labour between the police and the military does not work the same way in different parts of the world where there may be additional services (such as the gendarmerie, palace guards, or PMCs) who perform along the inside/outside boundary.

[9] Sociologist Julian Go (2024) starts from the same observation, but he is ultimately interested in understanding the militarisation of the police and the ways in which it has been tied up with racialisation in the US and UK.

[10] Please note that I do not offer a penultimate definition of militarism. This is intentional. I am interested in the spatio-temporal dynamics of the narrowing afor the men in unifond broadening of ISS definition of militarism and militarisation.

the military ways of doing things. The Cold War arms race between the superpowers and their respective blocs, and their economic reliance on arms sales to the rest of the world, in turn, is portrayed as a Cold War exigency whereby 'Europe' participated in the militarisation of other parts of the world, but was not marred by militarism itself. An important exception to this trend has been feminist research on the militarisation of women's lives and the broader society.

Let us consider an example. Rita Abrahamsen (2018: 2) has maintained that "at the time of independence, Africa seemed an unlikely site for militarism to flourish". This was because in the wake of anti-colonial struggle "[m]ost African political leaders and citizens were torn between distrust and disregard for the men in uniform". However, it all changed "within a short decade", wrote Abrahamsen, highlighting the roles played by international actors. Narrated as such, Abrahamsen's account goes against what we are accustomed to reading in ISS scholarship, where the local drivers of militarism in other parts of the world are viewed as innate even as the role played by the superpowers in its persistence is acknowledged. It is as if militarism was already there and what the superpowers did was only to exploit it for their purposes. In contrast, Abrahamsen (2018: 22) pointed out that while militarism "had its own internal agents" in Africa, it was not pre-given, but was learned in the Cold War context, at a time when the superpowers were looking for reliable local allies. Highlighting the role of North America and Western Europe in particular, Abrahamsen (2018: 22) has noted that "[f]or Africa's Western allies, functioning militaries…[were] regarded as naturally conservative institutions that could be relied upon to temper and contain the social pressures and dislocations arising from rapidly changing societies". But then, what was portrayed as "naturally conservative" behaviour on the part of the military had to be rendered as such through training, which was also offered by the external actors in the name of "the professionalisation of the army as part of building the modern nation-state" (Abrahamsen, 2018: 22). Militarism in Africa, Abrahamsen concluded, was "externally dependent and fuelled" by international actors.

The broader point being, it was not by their own accord that our contemporaries outside 'Europe' came to lead lives marred by militarism. They received expert guidance in developing and later maintaining their militarist ways. In some places such as Turkey and Brazil, such guidance went beyond the kind of 'dependence' and 'fuelling' of arms transfers and technical training that Abrahamsen observed in Africa, but included ideological training as well. In this case, then, the international in militarism was in the ways in which encouraging military rule elsewhere in the world allowed for the kind of 'stability' that the superpowers sought in lieu of international security. In those rare instances when ISS considered the international in militarism, this was solely in terms of the transfer of arms and technical training, and not in terms of the transfer of geopolitical ideas regarding the merits of military rule, as with Turkey where geopolitical ideas helped to depoliticise and naturalise the military's role in state governance (see, Bilgin, 2007, 2012b).

Most relevant for the purposes of this chapter is that by overlooking the international, students of ISS understood post-WWII dynamics inside 'Europe' in terms of the eradication of militarism, and outside in terms of its persistence.[11] Those participating in the militarisation of other parts of the world did not interpret their own condition as an instance of militarism. Cold War-fuelled arms races between the superpowers and their respective allies, and 'Europe's economic reliance on arms sales to other parts of the world, were understood as merely Cold War exigencies. As students of ISS presumed militarism to belong to a past world, they overlooked 'Europe's own agency in the emergence of militarism 'out there' and its lingering presence 'in here' (notwithstanding the availability of feminist insights, as highlighted above). The point being, (the study of) militarism in other parts of the world has been a 'constitutive outside' to (the study of) militarism inside 'Europe'. It is only by paying closer attention to the understandings of those who have experienced gendered (Åhäll, 2015; Enloe, 1983, 2000) and racialised (Go, 2024) insecurities at the hands of their own state and the police that we find out about what ISS scholars overlooked both inside and outside 'Europe'.

The International in Critical Approaches to Security

Over the years, while students of critical approaches to security made important progress in rethinking 'security', they have not always been interested in inquiring into the international in security. This comes across

---

[11] For a critique of ISS neglect of the study of militarism, see Selby and Stavrianakis (2013). For a study that acknowledged the international, but only in terms of arms transfers, see Thee (1977). Cynthia Enloe's (1990) *Bananas, Beaches and Bases* considered the international as central to the analysis of the militarisation of women's lives.

as somewhat surprising insofar as Ken Booth (1997, p. 95), one of the key authors of CSS, cited fellow scholars' lack of interest in how "other countries and other cultures–even enemies" thought about security as "a critical turning point" in his own search for alternatives. Writing at the height of the Cold War, Booth found a solution in area studies to help with inquiring into Soviet strategy and foreign policy.[12] However, as you will recall from Chapter 1, coupling the insights of area studies with conventional IR did not prove to be enough in addressing IR's Euro-centric limitations insofar as those insights were not brought to bear on IR concepts and theories. Rather, insecurities experienced in other parts of the world were studied in terms of the limitations of those actors and institutions, but not ISS concepts and theories. Critical approaches to security, too, have suffered a similar fate (Bilgin, 2016). While CSS scholars showed some awareness of the Eurocentric limitations of ISS, they treated the issue in terms of an 'absence'.

Let me clarify this point with the help of an illustration.[13] In *The Evolution of International Security Studies*, CSS scholars Buzan and Hansen (2009) identified the Eurocentrism of ISS as a problem.[14] Even as they registered Eurocentrism as a "blind spot" of the sub-field, the authors limited their task to analysing the evolution of the field "as it has taken place, not as we wish that it should have gone" (Buzan & Hansen, 2009: 19). Meaning that, in their study, the authors would focus on what was available in the disciplinary archives of ISS. The problem was that, at the time of their writing, students of ISS were aware of only a small body of scholarship that looked at insecurities experienced outside Western Europe and North America (see above). Was it even conceivable to write about the trajectory of ISS in a less Eurocentric manner, given the little record available in disciplinary archives? Buzan and Hansen thought not; hence their treatment of the issue as an 'absence'. Below, we will explore an alternative approach. In the remainder of this section, let us consider whether the Eurocentric limitations of ISS could be diagnosed as an 'absence'.

---

[12] Booth also authored one of the earliest studies on ethnocentrism in IR: *Strategy and Ethnocentrism* (1979).

[13] An early version of the following argument previously published in *Security Dialogue* (Bilgin, 2010) as part of a forum on Buzan and Hansen's book.

[14] The authors' preferred term is "Western-centrism".

First, those parts of the world other than 'Europe' were never absent from the study of security. As Bahgat Korany (1986) highlighted, they were there but slotted into one of two available roles (also see Barkawi & Laffey, 2006). They were either a part of the "established paradigm, and assigned the role of junior-partners in the power game" or they were labelled as "'trouble-makers", thriving on "nuisance power", fit for the exercise of techniques of "counterinsurgency" (Korany, 1986: 549). This was because ISS (as with IR, if you recall the discussion above) narrated international security from the perspective of those who wanted to maintain their position in a hierarchical world order. It is no wonder that ISS did not account for the insecurities of those who were supposed to be kept at bay.

Second, the issue is not (only) one of what can and cannot be found in the disciplinary archives of ISS. Following Tarak Barkawi (2016: 200), the issue is that "European histories of war provide the (provincial) basis for the putatively universal concepts and definitions with which we study war in both the global South and the North". ISS notions of statehood, nationhood and security have all been drawn from a particular narrative about "what is said to have happened" in 'Europe' (Grovogui, 2006: 1). Over the years, we have come to understand that these narratives were Eurocentric and that their Eurocentricity circumscribed our understanding of 'Europe' as well (Halperin, 1997).

But then, Third World critics of ISS were not always less Eurocentric (Bilgin, 2016). If you recall the difference between 'worlding as situatedness' and 'worlding as constitutive' from Chapter 2, Third World security scholars sought to capture the Eurocentric limits of ISS ISS through worlding the latter in terms of its geo-cultural situatedness. Accordingly, they failed to diagnose the constitutive effects of ISS on their own understanding of the world. As such, Third World security scholars also failed to reflect on how their analyses were Eurocentric in their anti-Eurocentrism (Wallerstein, 1997).

My fourth and final point is regarding "the problem of difference" (Inayatullah & Blaney, 2004), or how to make sense of difference given how "differently different" (Bilgin, 2012a) it may transpire to be. Where do we turn to, given that ISS has also prevailed outside 'Europe', and

Third World security scholars proved to be Eurocentric in their anti-Eurocentrism?[15] Elsewhere, I have argued that this is a question to be answered through inquiring into the agency of those policy-makers, analysts and IR scholars who were not merely vessels but also merchants in the adoption and utilisation of ISS concepts and theories outside North America and Western Europe (Bilgin, 2008, 2016). What ISS offered in the early years of the Cold War (a state-focused approach to world politics and 'national security' as the language of state action) also served the interests of elites outside North America and Western Europe, who were busy with state-building. They embraced the ISS notion of 'national security' and utilised it in building their own national security states. This is not to suggest they needed an ISS warrant. Nor is it to forget that throughout the Cold War there were policies in effect that actively encouraged the building of 'national security states' around the world. There is nevertheless a point to be made about the need for taking a reflexive look at the dynamics behind the presence of ISS (and CSS) outside 'Europe' notwithstanding the discipline's Eurocentric limitations (also see, Bilgin, 2011).

The broader point being, while the world outside 'Europe' has been left outside of ISS narratives, this does not translate into an 'absence' from world politics. Accordingly, the remedy cannot be found in inviting others to decolonise the study of security and/or address its racialised and/or gendered silences even as we overlook the scholarship of our coevals who have been asking the same questions as us but in another part of the world.[16] In what follows, I turn to the notion of 'constitutive outside' to see how those who have been outside of our ISS narratives have been constitutive of security in theory and in practice.

STUDYING THE 'CONSTITUTIVE OUTSIDE' OF SECURITY (STUDIES)

As discussed in Chapter 3, 'constitutive outside' refers to those who have been left out of (conventional and critical) narratives about the international. Yet, they have also been constitutive of 'Europe' insofar as those

---

[15] As you will see in the Postscript, this is what I found puzzling early on in my research.

[16] This is an issue also highlighted in Zvobgo et al. (2023).

ideas, practices, and institutions that are typically ascribed to 'Europe' do not have a single origin but multiple beginnings. Constitutive dynamics between 'Europe' and its outside have three aspects. First, providing bodies and lands whose labour and (material) riches were exploited by 'Europe'. This is the aspect that is better known and explored in the literature, especially in International Political Economy. Second, there is the self/other dynamics. This aspect has been explored by poststructuralist approaches to world politics. The third aspect, which is relatively under-explored, is learning, or about the ways in which ideas, practices and institutions that the literature has otherwise ascribed to 'Europe' have had multiple beginnings. In what follows, I will explore these three aspects with illustrations from ISS scholarship. This also serves to reiterate a point made before that what is lacking may not be 'knowledge' per se, but thinking globally so that we go looking for that 'knowledge' and bring it to bear on ISS concepts and theories.

Exploitative Dynamics: Mature Anarchy

While ISS and CSS acknowledge the usurpation of material resources that characterised the age of colonialism and imperialism, they are treated as historical background. Accordingly, the implications of those dynamics for contemporary world politics are overlooked. Here I look at the notion of 'mature anarchy' as an instance of failing to consider exploitative relations with the rest of the world as 'constitutive outside' to security in 'Europe'.

The notion of 'mature anarchy' was offered by Buzan (1991) in response to the question: 'Is international security possible?' While international security was not possible given the anarchical condition, argued Buzan, what was possible was to have pockets of 'mature anarchy', offering the experience of the European Community/Union as an example. In putting forward this argument, Buzan built on the distinction he had previously introduced in *People, States and Fear* (1983) between 'weak' and 'strong' states. Different from ISS which analysed states in terms of their material power alone, Buzan suggested that security scholars should also pay attention to 'strength' understood in terms of state-society relations. 'Mature anarchy' would not be possible without 'strong' states, argued Buzan. Given that the majority of states in the world maintained a tenuous relationship with their society, he concluded, international security is not possible.

How did we get to mature anarchy in the European Community/
Union? How was it that some states have come to be 'strong' and others
remained 'weak'? Buzan did not dwell on these questions.[17] He was not
alone in that a developmentalist narrative prevailed in the study of security,
presuming state 'strength' to be a product of innate characteristics.

In the late 1990s, scholars and policy-makers who identified 'state
failure' as a threat to international security concurred. They, too, were not
curious about the international political economic and security dynamics
within which some states 'succeed' or gain 'strength' and others 'fail'
or grow 'weak' (Bilgin & Morton, 2002). However, following Siba
Grovogui (2002: 329), the emergence of apparently 'successful' states in
'Europe' (such as Belgium) and 'failing' states elsewhere (as with Congo)
cannot be understood outside of exploitative relations insofar as "the
intra-European regime of sovereignty worked to the advantage of the
European entity while a permissive ethos in Africa undermined the consolidation of sovereign capacities in Congo". This is not only because of
imperialism and colonisation and the colonisers' usurpation of resources
in the colonies, although there is that in the case of Belgium and Congo's
dynamics. It is also because of the international society's 'differentiated
treatment' of both groups of states in that "while one regime contributed
to the 'resilience' of European quasi-states, another helped to undermine
the sovereignty of African entities and, later, to assist in the 'failure' of
a number of African states" (Grovogui, 2002: 316).[18] Then, exploitative
relations between 'Europe' and 'non-Europe' were not limited to usurpation of material resources alone. They were also constitutive of 'resilient'
states in 'Europe' and 'state failure' elsewhere.

The broader point being, so long as we are unable to make sense of
the security dynamics in the making of 'resilient' states in one part of
the world, we fall back on culturalist or other essentialist explanations for
the rest of the world. For instance, when Emanuel Adler and Michael
Barnett (1998) inquired into the making of a 'security community' in
Western Europe, they not only bracketed 'security' and focused on 'community', but also absented the international, thereby failing to account for

---

[17] As noted in Chapter 3, in his 2015 book with Lawson, Buzan (2015) offered a
more relational account of state development in the nineteenth century.

[18] You may recall from Chapter 2 that Grovogui first developed this argument in his
1996 book, *Sovereigns, Quasi-Sovereigns and Africans*.

the status of security communities elsewhere in the world.[19] Elsewhere, I explored gendered insecurities generated by the 2015 refugee crisis in the Mediterranean, highlighting that the persistence of women's insecurities in the Southeast of the Mediterranean is no mere cultural legacy. Rather, it is a product of policy collaboration between state level actors in the Northwest and the Southeast toward securing the flow of oil at reasonable prices for the former while maintaining regime stability for the latter group of states. Ensuring regime stability of the oil producing states and energy security for their allies in 'Europe' in turn, has generated gendered insecurities for women. The point being that the 'security community' located in the Northwest of the Mediterranean Sea has had a 'constitutive outside' in the Southeast (Bilgin, 2022).

Self/other Dynamics: Non-proliferation

Nuclear proliferation is one of the core issues for (the study of) international security. Scholarly and policy communities' unwavering focus on the advances that North Korea has made in their missile delivery systems, or the possibility of Iran developing its own nuclear weapon have been critiqued by CSS scholars as evidence of orientalisation (Biswas, 2018; Gusterson, 1999) and racialisation (Biswas, 2001; Mathur, 2020) of aspirant nuclear powers in (the study of) international security. Let us disentangle three dimensions of the self/other dynamics at work here.

First, there is the orientalised and racialised portrayal of the nuclear aspirations of those beyond the P5 (the five permanent members of the United Nations Security Council). The P5 developed their nuclear weapons well before the Non-Proliferation Treaty (NPT) was opened for signature in 1968. Hugh Gusterson (1999) explored the orientalist attitudes in the United States toward those who acquired or sought to acquire nuclear weapons after 1968. Identifying the main objections to the acquisition of nuclear weapons by non-nuclear states (such as Iran), or the apparently unsafe status of weapons in the new nuclear states (such as Pakistan), Gusterson showed that many if not all of these objections apply to the United States as well. The point being, there are no objective criteria by which to judge the propensity of some to safely acquire and manage nuclear weapons while others are viewed as

---

[19] Barkawi and Laffey (1999) advanced a similar line of critique of the democratic peace literature.

inherently untrustworthy. Hence Gusterson characterised (the study of) nuclear proliferation as shaped by self/other dynamics whereby the orientalised others' nuclear behaviour is portrayed as risky, while one's own policy is viewed as risk management.

Second, there is an unintended consequence of the NPT as identified by Shampa Biswas (2014). By way of limiting access to nuclear power status to the P5, argued Biswas, the NPT has generated what the author called a "nuclear desire" among the 'have nots'. Biswas suggested that the implementation of the NPT has kept alive the idea in the minds of new and aspirant nuclear powers that nuclear weapons are desirable for purposes of prestige as well as deterrence (also see, Mutimer, 2000). Writing in 1980 about 'Africa's nuclear future', Ali Mazrui (1980: 56) had advocated the nuclearisation in Africa on these very grounds when he argued that nuclearisation would mean "a new initiation, an important rite of passage, a recovery of adulthood. No longer will the Great Powers be permitted to say that such and such a weapon is 'not for Africans and children under 16'". The point being that the self/other dynamics work both ways; the NPT has proven counter-productive for the purposes of non-proliferation by way of keeping the promise of nuclear status a desirable option for 'have not' states.

Third, the self/other dynamics are also evident in the way in which students of ISS have come to accept the definition of international security as vertical proliferation for the P5, and threats to international security as horizontal proliferation by the others. While the critics have identified the threats posed by the P5's growing nuclear stockpile (including the budgets spent on producing, testing and maintaining them, and the risks of accidents and other environmental costs) they have not connected the dots, so to speak. ISS's portrayal of new and aspirant nuclear states as 'dangerous' others and the efforts spent in keeping them 'outside' the nuclear club has been constitutive of this particular definition of international security as maintaining vertical proliferation for the P5.

Ideational Dynamics: Arms Control Norms

Eurocentric narratives about ideas having a single origin (as opposed to multiple beginnings, see Chapter 3) have shaped the horizons of students of security as to who can produce 'knowledge' and who gets to receive it. Consider the case of those narratives on arms control norms which portray 'Europe' as the producer of ideas and the rest of the world as unwilling recipients.[20] In what follows, I will suggest that the difficulties encountered in getting others to value arms control norms can be located in our Eurocentric limitations insofar as ISS narrates the history of norms development as one of autonomous development in and by 'Europe'. Inquiring into the 'constitutive outside' of these norms, in turn, reveals ideational dynamics that are missing from the said narratives.

Following Keith Krause and Andrew Latham's study on the history of arms control, what is portrayed by ISS as a 'Western arms control culture' is in fact a particular set of norms that was developed in interaction with others during the Cold War. In this case, those others who were left outside the ISS narratives are the Second World or 'the East'. According to Krause and Latham (2012: 45), it was through interaction and nego-tiation that a "shared understanding that the East–West security dilemma needed to be addressed cooperatively" was created. The point here being that the 'East' served not merely as an 'other' to the 'Western' 'self' in the development of arms control norms, but helped constitute them.

Highlighting the Second World as a 'constitutive outside' to what is portrayed as the 'Western arms control culture' is no mere academic point. It is essential for the effort to encourage arms control practices in other parts of the world, as also underscored by Krause and Latham (2012). The problem here has four consequences, two of which are already identified by the authors. First, such a self-image of themselves as norms producer disinclines policy-makers in North America and Western Europe from reflecting on their presumption of the 'West' as "having a natural vocation to act as a 'benign hegemon' in global security affairs" (Krause & Latham, 2012: 41). Such a presumption, in turn, has impli-cations for their own goal of promoting arms control in other parts of the world. The second and related consequence identified by Krause and Latham (2012: 41) is that "it predisposes representatives of Western states to believe that non-Western states are less well suited to play a lead role in global security issues."[21] Let me add a third one: it predisposes policy-makers in other parts of the world to believe that these norms have nothing to do with them, thereby giving them an easy out in cases of

---

[20] For a similar discussion on conflict resolution and mediation 'expertise', see Bilgin (2019).

[21] This is an issue explored in Bilgin and Herz (2023).

violations. Fourth, it leaves no sense of ownership for those who do want to follow norms.

Thinking globally about security cannot stop at exploring practices in other parts of the world as if they have had no contribution to (the study of) security. But then, CSS has not always fared better than ISS in this regard. During the Cold War, the calls for nuclear disarmament and arms control were first voiced by anti-nuclear protesters and 'radical' scholars who amplified their insecurities. At the time, anti-nuclear activism was a transnational phenomenon spearheaded by the Campaign for Nuclear Disarmament (CND), African liberation movements, and the civil rights movement in the US (Allman, 2008). In making a case for decentring the state in (the study of) security, CSS scholars drew on the experiences of anti-nuclear activists of the Cold War years (Bilgin et al., 1998; Booth, 1997). That our narratives on CSS seldom feature the roles played by anti-nuclear activists in the evolution of critical approaches to security does not mean that they were 'absent'. To repeat the point above in a slightly different way, considering insecurities as well as activism in other parts of the world as 'constitutive outside' to security has potential consequences for not only the scholarly world but also policy-making.

CONCLUSION

This chapter inquired into the question how to think globally about security. When ISS (and CSS) narratives fail to account for the international in security, it is tempting to turn to others and ask, 'so, what do you think?' My discussion in this chapter took us in a different direction, seeking to highlight how those who are absented from ISS and CSS narratives are at the same time the 'constitutive outside' of what is otherwise presented as autonomously produced in/by 'Europe'. Let me reiterate a point that I made earlier: Eurocentrism is not only about the situatedness of ideas and institutions, but also about their constitutive effects. It circumscribes our horizons as to who can produce 'knowledge' about (international) security and who needs to receive such 'knowledge'. The implication is that thinking globally about security cannot be limited to decentring, leaving untouched those approaches who presume that ideas and practices in other parts of the world have had no contribution to ISS (or CSS).

BIBLIOGRAPHY

Abrahamsen, R. (2018). Return of The Generals? Global Militarism in Africa From the Cold War To the Present. *Security Dialogue, 49*(1–2), 19–31.

Adler, E., & Barnett, M. N. (Eds.). (1998). *Security Communities*. Cambridge University Press.

Åhäll, L. (2015). The Hidden Politics of Militarization and Pop Culture as Political Communication. *E-International Relations*. https://www.e-ir.info/2015/05/16/the-hidden-politics-of-militarization-and-pop-culture-as-political-communication/

Al-Mashat, A. M. M. (1985). *National Security in the Third World*. Westview Press.

Allman, J. (2008). Nuclear Imperialism and the Pan-African Struggle for Peace and Freedom: Ghana, 1959–1962. *Souls, 10*(2), 83–102.

Altınay, A. G. (2004). *The Myth of The Military Nation: Militarism, Gender, and Education in Turkey*. Palgrave Macmillan.

Ayoob, M. (1995). *The Third World Security Predicament: State Making, Regional Conflict, and The International System*. Lynne Rienner Publishers.

Ayoob, M. (Ed.). (1986). *Regional Security in the Third World: Case Studies from Southeast Asia and the Middle East*. Westview Press.

Azar, E. E., & Moon, C.-I. (Eds.) (1988). *National Security in the Third World: The Management of Internal and External Threats*. Palgrave.

Barkawi, T. (2016). Decolonising War. *European Journal of International Security, 1*(2), 199–214.

Barkawi, T., & Laffey, M. (1999). The Imperial Peace: Democracy, Force and Globalization. *European Journal of International Relations, 5*(4), 403–434.

Barkawi, T., & Laffey, M. (2006). The Postcolonial Moment in Security Studies. *Review of International Studies, 32*(2), 329–352.

Ben-Eliezer, U. (1997). Rethinking The Civil-Military Relations Paradigm: The Inverse Relation Between Militarism and Praetorianism Through the Example of Israel. *Comparative Political Studies, 30*(3), 356–374.

Bilgin, P. (2007). "Only Strong States Can Survive in Turkey's Geography": The Uses of "Geopolitical Truths" in Turkey. *Political Geography, 26*(7), 740–756.

Bilgin, P. (2008). Thinking Past 'Western' IR? *Third World Quarterly, 29*(1), 5–23.

Bilgin, P. (2010). The 'Western-Centrism' of Security Studies: 'Blind Spot' Or Constitutive Practice? *Security Dialogue, 41*(6), 615.

Bilgin, P. (2011). The Politics of Studying Securitization? The Copenhagen School in Turkey. *Security Dialogue, 42*(4–5), 399–412.

Bilgin, P. (2012a). Security in the Arab World and Turkey: Differently Different. In A. Tickner & D. Blaney (Eds.), *Thinking International Relations Differently* (pp. 27–47). Routledge.

Bilgin, P. (2012b). Turkey's 'Geopolitics Dogma.' In S. Guzzini (Ed.), *Fixing Foreign Policy Identity: 1989 and the Uneven Revival of Geopolitical Thought in Europe* (pp. 151–173). Cambridge University Press.

Bilgin, P. (2016). *The International in Security, Security in The International*. Routledge.

Bilgin, P. (2019). Worlding Conflict Resolution and Mediation Expertise: In the 'Global South.' In A. Leander & O. Waever (Eds.), *Assembling Exclusive Expertise: Knowledge, Ignorance and Conflict Resolution in the Global South* (pp. 77–92). Routledge.

Bilgin, P. (2021). On the 'Does Theory Travel?' Question: Traveling With Edward Said. In Z. G. Çapan, F. Dos Reis, & M. Grasten (Eds.), *The Politics of Translation in International Relations* (pp. 245–255). Springer.

Bilgin, P. (2022). The 'Migrant Crisis in The Mediterranean' As A Threat to Women's Security in the EU? A Contrapuntal Reading. *Geopolitics, 27*(3), 773–790.

Bilgin, P., Booth, K., & Wyn Jones, R. (1998). Security Studies: The Next Stage? *Naçao E Defesa, 84*, 137–157.

Bilgin, P., & Morton, A. D. (2002). Historicising Representations of 'Failed States': Beyond the Cold-War Annexation of The Social Sciences? *Third World Quarterly, 23*(1), 55–80.

Bilgin, P., & Herz, M. (2023). *Who Speaks Security (in the Name of the International Community)?* Paper Presented at the International Studies Association Annual Conference, Montreal, Canada.

Biswas, S. (2001). "Nuclear Apartheid" As Political Position: Race As A Postcolonial Resource? *Alternatives: Global, Local, Political, 26*(4), 485–522.

Biswas, S. (2014). *Nuclear Desire: Power and the Postcolonial Nuclear Order*. University of Minnesota Press.

Biswas, S. (2018). Iran v 'the International Community': A Postcolonial Analysis of the Negotiations on the Iranian Nuclear Program. *Asian Journal of Political Science, 26*(3), 331–351.

Booth, K. (1979). *Strategy and Ethnocentrism*. Holmes and Meier.

Booth, K. (1997). Security and Self: Reflections of A Fallen Realist. In K. Krause & M. C. Williams (Eds.), *Critical Security Studies: Concepts and Cases* (pp. 83–119). University of Minnesota Press.

Buzan, B. (1983). *People, States and Fear: The National Security Problem in International Relations*. University of North Carolina Press.

Buzan, B. (1991). Is International Security Possible? In K. Booth (ed.), New Thinking about Strategy and International Security, (pp. 31–55). Harper Collins.

Buzan, B., & Hansen, L. (2009). *The Evolution of International Security Studies*. Cambridge University Press.

Buzan, B., & Lawson, G. (2015). *The Global Transformation: History, Modernity and The Making of International Relations*. Cambridge University Press.

Cardoso, F. H., & Faletto, E. (1979). *Dependency and Development in Latin America*. University of California Press.

Chan, S. (2021). *African Political Thought: An Intellectual History of the Quest for Freedom*. Hurst Publishers.

Diamint, R. (2015). A New Militarism in Latin America. *Journal of Democracy, 26*, 155.

Donnelly, J. (2006). Sovereign Inequalities and Hierarchy in Anarchy: American Power and International Society. *European Journal of International Relations, 12*(2), 139–170.

Du Bois, W. E. B. (1946). *Color and Democracy: Colonies and Peace*. Harcourt Brace Co.

Eastwood, J. (2018). Rethinking Militarism as Ideology: The Critique of Violence After Security. *Security Dialogue, 49*, 44–56.

Enloe, C. (1983). *Does Khaki Become You? The Militarisation of Women's Lives*: South End Pr.

Enloe, C. (1990). *Bananas, Beaches and Bases: Making Feminist Sense of International Politics*. University of California Press.

Enloe, C. (1996). Margins, Silences and Bottom Rungs: How To Overcome The Underestimation of Power in the Study of International Relations. In K. Booth, S. Smith, & M. Zalewski (Eds.), *International Theory: Positivism and Beyond* (pp. 186–202). Cambridge University Press.

Enloe, C. (2000). *Maneuvers: The International Politics of Militarizing Women's Lives*. University of California Press.

Go, J. (2024). *Policing Empires: Militarization, Race, and the Imperial Boomerang in Britain and the US*. Oxford University Press.

Grovogui, S. N. (2002). Regimes of Sovereignty: International Morality and the African Condition. *European Journal of International Relations, 8*(3), 315–338.

Grovogui, S. N. (2006). *Beyond Eurocentrism and Anarchy: Memories of International Order and Institutions*. Palgrave Macmillan.

Gusterson, H. (1999). Nuclear Weapons and the Other in the Western Imagination. *Cultural Anthropology, 14*(1), 111–143.

Halperin, S. (1997). *In the Mirror of the Third World: Capitalist Development in Modern Europe*. Cornell University Press.

Hobson, J. M., & Sharman, J. C. (2005). The Enduring Place of Hierarchy in World Politics: Tracing The Social Logics of Hierarchy and Political Change. *European Journal of International Relations, 11*(1), 63–98.

Inayatullah, N., & Blaney, D. L. (2004). *International Relations and the Problem of Difference*. Routledge.

Kissinger, H. A. (1958). Nuclear Testing and the Problem of Peace. *Foreign Affairs, 37*(1), 1–18.

Korany, B. (1986). Strategic Studies and the Third World: A Critical Evaluation. *International Social Science Journal, 38*(4), 547–562.

Krause, K., & Latham, A. (2012). Constructing Non-Proliferation and Arms Control: The Norms of Western Practice. In *Culture and Security* (pp. 23–54). Routledge.

Mann, M. (1987). The Roots and Contradictions of Modern Militarism. *New Left Review, 162*(2), 27–55.

Mathur, R. (2020). *Civilizational Discourses in Weapons Control.* Springer.

Mazrui, A. (1980). Africa's Nuclear Future. *Survival, 22*(2), 76–79.

Mccoy, A. (2016). Capillaries of Empire: Colonial Pacification and The Origins of US Global Surveillance. In J. Hönke & M.-M. Müller (Eds.), *The Global Making of Policing: Postcolonial Perspectives* (pp. 20–39). Routledge.

Mutimer, D. (2000). *The Weapons State: Proliferation and The Framing of Security*: Lynne Rienner Publishers.

Neocleous, M. (2013). The Dream of Pacification: Accumulation, Class War, and The Hunt. *Socialist Studies/Études Socialistes, 9*(2), 7–31.

Selby, J., & Stavrianakis, A. (Eds.). (2013). *Militarism and International Relations: Political Economy, Security and Theory.* Routledge.

Sharp, J. P. (2013). Geopolitics at the Margins? Reconsidering Genealogies of Critical Geopolitics. *Political Geography, 37*, 20–29.

Sylvester, C. (1994). *Feminist Theory and International Relations in a Postmodern Era.* Cambridge University Press.

Thee, M. (1977). Militarism and Militarization in Contemporary International Relations. *Bulletin of Peace Proposals, 8*(4), 296–309.

Thomas, C. (1991). New Directions in Thinking About Security in the Third World. In K. Booth (Ed.), *New Thinking About Strategy and International Security* (pp. 267–289). Harper Collins.

Vitalis, R. (2005). Birth of a Discipline. In D. Long & B. C. Schmidt (Eds.), *Imperialism and Internationalism in the Discipline of International Relations* (pp. 159–181). State University of New York Press.

Wallerstein, I. (1974). Dependence in an Interdependent World: The Limited Possibilities of Transformation Within the Capitalist World Economy. *African Studies Review, 17*, 1–26.

Wallerstein, I. (1997). Eurocentrism and Its Avatars: The Dilemmas of Social Science. *New Left Review*(I/226), 93–108.

Wendt, A., & Friedheim, D. (2009). Hierarchy Under Anarchy: Informal Empire and The East German State. *International Organization, 49*(04), 689.

Zvobgo, K., Sotomayor, A. C., Rublee, M. R., Loken, M., Karavas, G., & Duncombe, C. (2023). Race and Racial Exclusion in Security Studies: A Survey of Scholars. *Security Studies, 32*(4-5), pp. 593–621.

CHAPTER 5

Thinking Globally About (the Study of) Foreign Policy

Karen Smith

Abstract This chapter asks how we might think globally about (the study of) foreign policy. One of the most significant questions that arises is whether or not to assume difference in the way in which the international is experienced, understood and enacted in different parts of the world. After a brief overview of criticism of the Eurocentric biases and assumptions that have traditionally shaped both Foreign Policy Analysis (FPA) and the broader study of foreign policy, the chapter turns to existing attempts at addressing Eurocentrism by outlining some of the different approaches taken by scholars. The final section applies a relational approach to understanding South Africa's foreign policy, focusing in particular on the notion of relational circles, and reflects on questions and insights raised by this case.

Keywords Foreign policy analysis (FPA) · Eurocentrism · Relationality · South Africa · Decentring · Decolonising

© The Author(s), under exclusive license to Springer Nature
Switzerland AG 2024
P. Bilgin and K. Smith, *Thinking Globally About World Politics: Beyond Global IR*, https://doi.org/10.1007/978-3-031-56572-4_5

Introduction

In the discussions about efforts to address IR's Eurocentric limitations, relatively little has been said about Foreign Policy Analysis (FPA) specifically, as well as the study of foreign policy more generally. One could ask whether Chris Alden and Amnon Aran's comment that, while the analytical frameworks used in FPA draw heavily on systemic IR theories such a neorealism,[1] the lack of systematic engagement between IR and FPA has meant that FPA has failed "to adequately engage with critical intellectual developments in IR over the last two decades" (2012: 110) still holds true. What is indisputable is that the relationship between IR and FPA remains an ambiguous one.[2] Regardless of where one stands in this debate, in practice much of the work that is done by IR scholars in fact focuses on foreign policy, albeit not always in the form of FPA *per se*. In fact, based on the annual International Studies Association (ISA) convention programmes, FPA is one of the two largest subfields of IR (together with International Security Studies). It is also generally the most prominent subfield of IR in the Global South, and scholars from the Global South are, ironically, often criticised for confusing foreign policy with IR.[3] The rationale behind this chapter is therefore that the study of foreign policy forms an integral part of the field of IR, and that the ontological, epistemological and methodological questions we grapple with in thinking globally about world politics are equally relevant to the study of foreign policy. Following the introduction, the next part of the chapter provides an overview of attempts at addressing Eurocentrism in FPA and foreign policy studies (FPS). The final section applies a relational approach to understanding South Africa's foreign policy.

I deliberately distinguish between FPA and FPS as I understand the former to refer to a particular sub-discipline that is heavily US foreign policy-centric and entails the use of specific methods of analysis–often quantitative and involving formal modelling. What I refer to as FPS,

---

[1] While Waltz's structural neorealism is essentially a theory of the international system, it has been used primarily by scholars and practitioners to explain the foreign policy decisions of individual states.

[2] See Hellmann and Jorgensen (2015) for an exploration of the relationship between foreign policy analysis and IR theory.

[3] See the reference in Chapter 2 to Hoffman's (1977) comment that IR scholars in the United States mistook their foreign policy interests for IR.

on the other hand, is a much wider endeavour that can but need not include research drawing on FPA models. Valerie Hudson (2015) cited Steve Smith, Amelia Hadfield and Tim Dunne as stating, "[t]o treat FPA as the only approach to the study of foreign policy would limit our discussions," implying that it can also take the form of, for example, a more descriptive approach to understanding the foreign policy environments, actors and influences of (mostly but not exclusively) state actors. Gilbert Khadiagala and Terrence Lyons' 2001 edited volume on African foreign policies is exemplary of the latter. With a focus on the foreign policy context and the constraints imposed by the external and domestic environments as well as the actors that shape foreign policy, none of the chapters delve into the decision-making process or apply existing models of FPA. Korwa Adar and Rok Ajulu (2002) and Adar and Peter Schraeder's (2007) edited volumes on Southern and East African foreign policy respectively, follow the same approach. With very few exceptions, the case studies are all predominantly descriptive, outlining the relevant actors, policy priorities, and the contours of the domestic, regional and international foreign policy context with little or no theoretical engagement. There is no attempt to read the cases through existing FPA models or theories, nor to suggest alternative analytical or theoretical lenses through which to do so.

Indeed, the study of foreign policy is much more widespread not only in the Global South but also in other non-North American settings. As Sumit Ganguly and Manjeet Pardesi (2015: 57) argued in their overview of foreign policy analysis in India, "the study of FPA as a subfield of the academic discipline of international relations (IR) is largely absent in India. This is not to suggest that the study of foreign policy is absent in India." Raymond Hinnebusch (2015: 77), in writing on FPA and the Arab World, made the same point: "While writings on the foreign policies of Arab states are by no means scarce, the literature that explicitly uses the analytical tools of foreign policy analysis (FPA) is more limited." In some variants, for example in Europe, the study of foreign policy is often closer to IR, drawing on IR theories in its exploration of foreign policy.[4]

[4] See for example, Hadfield and Hudson (2015).

Providing a detailed overview of the development of the sub-field of FPA, and FPS more generally is beyond the scope of this chapter.[5] Instead, the focus is more on how we might move on from here: how might we think globally about (the study of) foreign policy? Nevertheless, to provide some context, I turn briefly to some criticism of the Eurocentric biases and assumptions that have traditionally shaped both FPA and FPS (which I collectively refer to as the study of foreign policy) while marginalising and silencing voices from outside North America and Western Europe.

Branwen Gruffyd-Jones' 2006 critique of the Eurocentric and imperial nature of IR is equally relevant to the study of foreign policy, and includes the lack of recognition of the continued impact of colonialism and imperialism on what drives foreign policy in many parts of the world. The way in which actors in the Global South view and experience the international, and conduct their international relations through, amongst others, foreign policy, cannot be understood in the absence of these ever-present processes that continue to influence relations. One of the main criticisms of the study of foreign policy is the privileging of international anarchy as the systemic condition of foreign policy, and the reliance on juridical notions of sovereignty. Such assumptions serve to underplay or dismiss the hierarchical relations of power and structural constraints that Global South states face in foreign policy making, and fail to recognize the continued power of historical constraints (Çalkivik, 2020: 202). As a result, "the prevailing models of foreign policy have surreptitiously validated a particular ethos of international relations by elevating them into universal categories" (Grovogui, 2003: 40) and fail to consider alternative explanations. In particular, they are based on assumptions of individualism and rationalism as the underlying drivers of action and therefore prioritise explanations based on particular understandings of what constitutes interests, specifically that interests are always individualist.[6] Some criticism addresses Eurocentrism in FPS more generally, while other concerns are directed specifically at the US-centric nature of FPA (also see the discussion in Chapter 2 about US hegemony in IR).

---

[5] There are many texts that already do this. See, for example, Çalkivik (2020), Smith et al. (2016).

[6] This differs from alternative understandings of interest provided by relational approaches, for example the idea of interests-in-relations that will be elaborated on below.

ADDRESSING EUROCENTRISM IN THE STUDY OF FOREIGN POLICY

In considering how to think globally about foreign policy, as with world politics more generally, one of the most significant questions that arises is whether or not to assume difference in the way in which the international is experienced, understood and enacted in different parts of the world. Relatedly, are foreign policy theories, as mid-level theories, essentially different to IR theories? Are we therefore more likely to accept the idea that a theory of Chinese foreign policy might differ substantially from a theory of US foreign policy rather than that we need a Chinese theory of IR? One's answer to this will have a direct influence on what one sees as promising avenues to think differently about foreign policy. Below I will outline some of the different approaches taken by scholars. The aim is not to set these different positions up as one being better than the others, but rather in terms of how they think about difference between states based on assumed geocultural characteristics, particularly between states in the Global South and the Global North or 'Europe' and the rest. First, some scholars either do not recognise difference or rather do not regard it as important to understanding foreign policy. While they claim to be interested in pluralising IR and making it more inclusive, they are still operating with Eurocentric assumptions about the universality of existing foreign policy theories and frameworks. Second, others focus on the inappropriateness of Eurocentric concepts and theories to the Global South arguing that the study of foreign policy needs to be decentred. At the same time, however, they do not question that these analytical frameworks are also relevant for understanding European foreign policy. Thirdly, there are those who assume that, while states in the Global North and Global South may have some differences, they are also still similar in many ways, and therefore existing theories and frameworks are relevant for both, potentially with some adjustments. A fourth group of scholars emphasise particularity, based on the assumption that Global South states are essentially different and that this requires the application of different analytical frameworks, including drawing on local ideas and concepts. Going beyond the question of difference or similarity, postcolonial approaches problematise the way in which what constitutes understandings of foreign policy are themselves a product of Eurocentric assumptions about the nature of statehood and the international. Finally, in their emphasis on interconnectedness, and the mutual constitution of self and other, some relational approaches view similarity and difference as being two sides of the same coin, rather than contradictory.[7]

Assuming Universality: Widening the Universe of Cases

If we assume that states everywhere are essentially similar, then it follows that it is possible to apply what are presumed to be universal theoretical frameworks. In a special issue exploring the "boundedness of foreign policy analysis theory", Klaus Brummer and Valerie Hudson (2017: 157) for example, contended that "the explanation of foreign policy making beyond North America does not require an entirely new or different set of analytical tools".[8] Following on from this, in a 2021 special issue of *International Affairs* on "new directions in foreign policy analysis", Brummer (2021) proposed that FPA could be advanced by looking beyond the US context to instead studying foreign policy makers in the Global South. While this approach is essentially one of pluralising the cases studied beyond the USA and Europe, most of these contributions remain constrained in that they apply instead of challenge dominant frameworks. When the frameworks do not fit the case, instead of being puzzled, the assumption is that the case is an exception or an aberration, rather than that the problem might lie with the framework. The call also underplays the fact that a vast literature exists on foreign policy of the Global South,[9] much of it by scholars in the Global South, who have largely been ignored by US-centric FPA scholars. Brummer and Hudson's 2015 edited volume, which presents an overview of FPA beyond North America, is an exception. The chapters take the form of literature reviews of the development of FPS (and less FPA) in different states in predominantly the Global

---

[7] At the same time, when scholars tie relationality to particular geo-cultural contexts, they can perpetuate assumptions of difference.

[8] In a footnote (2017: 165, footnote 40), they admit that there may be some cognitive bias involved in applying FPA models that could influence the conclusion that "FPA theory travels better to non-North American settings than we would have originally expected." 2017: 165)

[9] While it is beyond the scope of this chapter to list work on the foreign policies of individual states, some volumes that include chapters on different states in the Global South include: Braveboy-Wagner (2003), Brummer and Hudson (2015); on African states, Clapham (1977), Khadiagala and Lyons (2001); on Arab states, Korany and Desouki (2008), Hinnebusch and Ehteshami (2014).

South, although Western Europe is also included. While, in the conclusion, Brummer argues that the growing body of non-North American FPA research "has extended FPA geographically, conceptually and theoretically, and empirically" (2015: 169–170) with one or two exceptions, the book mainly showcases the geographical and empirical, and stops short of pointing to potentially fruitful avenues of thinking differently about foreign policy that go beyond largely descriptive work.

The charge that foreign policy studies being done in the Global South are inferior due to the fact that they are a-theoretical[10] is also implicit in the suggestion that "moving past descriptive works to a more avowedly theoretical orientation would facilitate the search for less North American-bounded FPA theory" (Brummer, 2015: 184). Numerous problematic assumptions underlie these statements. These include prejudices about what constitutes 'knowledge'[11] and theory, and which methodological approaches are preferable. These in turn are based on underlying assumptions about epistemological questions concerning how we can gain 'knowledge' about foreign policy (only through formal modelling methods, for example). In summary, the implication that foreign policy scholars from the Global South should best adapt their work to meet the standards of North-American FPA comes across as patronising at best. In this regard, Patrick Chabal and Jean-Pascal Daloz's (2006) warning that employing a pre-existing conceptual framework and research questions can undermine recognizing difference and impose a Eurocentric view of the world on the subject being studied, comes to mind.

Both Similar and Different

If we assume that there are both similarities and differences between the foreign policies of states in the Global North and the Global South, then adapting existing theories and concepts to make them more relevant to different contexts could be seen as a fruitful way of thinking globally

---

[10] Also see the discussion in Chapter 2 on the presumed 'absence' of theory in and from the Global South.

[11] 'Knowledge' here refers to what are assumed to be legitimate forms of knowledge, based on Eurocentric assumptions about the superiority of particular epistemic traditions, which are regarded as scientific and universal, while other forms of knowledge are relegated to being unscientific, traditional, and irrational.

about foreign policy. In his overview of FPA and the Arab world, for example, Hinnebusch (2015: 99) notes that

> the traditions developed in North America have been successfully imported, with the same categories and issues typically addressed. They have also been adapted to the MENA region where, for example, the role of dependency, identity, and personalized leadership appears more salient than elsewhere. Arab scholars of foreign policy have chosen from the repertoire of North American approaches and have internalized many of the methods and approaches most appropriate for understanding their countries.

Scholars whose work in this regard has been recognised by the fringes of IR include Mohammed Ayoob's (2002) study on subaltern realism, in which he considered how ongoing state-building processes in Global South states shapes their foreign policy, and Carlos Escude (1998), whose peripheral realism emphasised that the international system can best be understood as a hierarchy rather than an anarchy, and also called for greater attention to socio-political contexts in the Global South.[12]

Less well known are the South African scholars who, in the late 1990s and early 2000s, engaged with the existing literature on middle power theory in IR that had been developed predominantly by Canadian scholars like Andrew Cooper and Robert Cox. Not only does this constitute a refinement or adaptation of US-centric FPA theories and models as the examples above, but it builds on an underlying recognition that FPA is also inappropriate for understanding the foreign policy of states like Canada or Norway (and therefore necessitating the development of mid-level theories like middle power theory), let alone states in the Global South. This underlines the distinction between US- and Euro-centrism. Questioning the applicability of the concept of middle power—initially reserved for traditional, northern middle powers like Canada, Australia, Norway and Sweden—South African scholars like Maxi Schoeman (2000) and Eduard Jordaan (2003) subsequently made an important contribution to the literature by developing the concept through providing greater analytical clarity, and specifically making the

---

[12] For a recent revisiting of peripheral realism, see Schenoni and Escude (2016). For examples of other hybrid concepts used in Latin American foreign policy studies, see Giacolone (2015).

distinction between traditional and new, emergent or emerging middle powers that recognized their similarities but at the same time highlighted their differences (Smith, 2018:84). The work of these scholars is an illustration of how an existing concept can be adapted in order to make it more applicable to a particular context—in this case, understanding the role that South Africa was playing in the world. Significantly, however, their modification is not only useful for understanding South Africa but applies to a much wider group of states that all fit the criteria of "emerging middle powers".

While adjusting existing frameworks and concepts to make them more appropriate to cases in the Global South is one approach to thinking globally about world politics, it can also be criticised as being limited in its ability to challenge the continued dominance of Eurocentric approaches as it continues to use them and dominant framings of what constitutes foreign policy as a basis. Relatedly, such strategies of adaptation do not engage with the deeply entrenched Eurocentric assumptions that underlie existing theories and concepts (also see the discussion in Chapter 1 on the failure of Area studies to revisit IR concepts).

Particularity: Emphasising Difference

If one believes that the nature of foreign policy making in the Global South is fundamentally different from that of states in the Global North, both in terms of decision-making practices and the internal and external factors that influence them, this would require alternative theoretical models to explain these differences. To paraphrase Benjamin Herborth (2015: 101) this would necessitate "195 theories of foreign policy". The criticism that the US-centrism of existing FPA models is clearly exposed when they are applied to non-US contexts is a common one that forms part of a long-standing view that existing approaches are wholly unsuitable to understanding foreign policy making in the Global South. John Clark (2001: 71), for example, notes that "...most common foreign policy models designed to explain decision-making in developed states are inadequate to explain the decisions in African states."

From these perspectives, dominant, US-centric and Eurocentric narratives that are based on particular histories and experiences of 'Europe',[13]

---

[13] As noted in Chapter 1, the 'Europe' of Eurocentrism is not a location on a physical map but a mental map, and includes Western Europe and North America.

and/or myths about the particularity of what is regarded as 'Europe', often blind us to the motivations and objectives of actors in the Global South. The result is that analysts drawing on FPS frameworks are often stumped by their inability to explain certain foreign policy decisions on the basis of interest-based calculations that may make sense (but also not in all cases) from a US or Western European perspective. In his 1986 volume on foreign policy in the third world, Bahgat Korany emphasised the importance of "state-societal" and "global-systemic" factors to understanding foreign policy making in these parts of the world. In their edited volume on African foreign policy, Gilbert Khadiagala and Terrence Lyons (2001: 3) note the importance of studying the severe structural constraints and the legacy of colonialism facing many postcolonial states in their foreign policy making. Christopher Clapham (1977) makes this point even more forcefully, arguing that the imperatives of regime and state survival translate into foreign policy actions that aim at maximising political and economic resources from the external environment in order to subdue domestic threats, while at the same time there is a desire to enact an independent foreign policy free of external interference. The international environment is thus seen as being both a constraining and enabling factor. In addition, the regional dimension has become increasingly significant in understanding the context in which African foreign policy is made (see for example, Adar, 2015).

The study of China's foreign policy has been a major focus of the 'globalising turn'[14] (see the discussion in Chapter 3 on 'non-Western IR'). 'IR with Chinese characteristics' started off as a project to think the world through Chinese eyes, with foreign policy experts using some of the insights to argue that due to China's particular history and culture, one cannot understand the Chinese worldview, and by extension Chinese foreign policy behaviour, from a 'Western IR' perspective. Unlike scholars such as John Mearsheimer, who hold that China's behaviour can best be understood using structural realist theory, the contention is that, instead, the influence of for example Confucianism, Daoism and Buddhism, and the very different philosophical foundations cannot be neglected in analysing Chinese foreign policy. In line with this view, making sense of

---

[14] We use 'globalising turn' to refer to the effort spearheaded by Amitav Acharya since 2014. The body of scholarship seeking to address IR's Eurocentric limitations has a much longer history.

the foreign policies of the Global South thus requires novel and context-specific analytical tools,[15] which could take the form of new concepts or theories.

Beyond adapting existing concepts and theories to local conditions (as discussed in the previous section) some concepts from indigenous cultural-philosophical traditions have been employed to analyse foreign policy in certain parts of the world. In the case of China, scholars have focused on the concept of *tianxia*, literally translated as "all-under-heaven" to make sense of the country's foreign policy. Scholars such as Tingyang Zhao (2009, 2021)[16] have shown how, in rejecting the West-phalian territorial states system, tianxia instead sees the world as a single political space. The concept is also of particular importance for under-standing China's foreign policy, having been revived by contemporary Chinese IR scholars for the purpose of rethinking China's role in the world.[17]

In relation to India, Ganguly and Pardesi (2015) highlight two concepts—*Panchsheel* and non-alignment—that have influenced foreign policy making in the country. While the motivation behind the idea of non-alignment was an independent foreign policy rather than a position of isolation or neutrality, *Panchsheel*—elaborated in five principles[18]—was proposed as an alternative framework for the conduct of international relations, with the aim of ensuring international peace and develop-ment. While neither concept has been the subject of rigorous theoretical development, both are useful not only for understanding India's foreign relations, but foreign policy more widely.[19] Non-alignment in particular holds much potential as a lens through which to view the foreign poli-cies of actors in the Global South, particularly in light of its apparent revitalisation and invocation in relation to Russia's war against Ukraine.[20]

---

[15] It should be noted that some scholars like L. H. M. Ling draw on the same worldviews and philosophical influences to make a more universalist argument.

[16] For a critical overview of Zhao's work on *tianxia*, See Callahan (2008).

[17] For an exploration of some of the practical implications of a Chinese foreign policy inspired by *tianxia*, see Bell (2017).

[18] Mutual respect for each other's territorial integrity and sovereignty; nonaggression; noninterference in each other's internal affairs; equality and mutual benefit; and peaceful coexistence (MEA, n.d.).

[19] See, for example, de Coning et al. (2015)

[20] See, for example, Fortin et al. (2023)

The concept of autonomy also offers a different lens for thinking about foreign policy than those available in mainstream IR. Tickner (2014: 82) adds that "Latin American readings of autonomy constitute one of the region's most interesting and noteworthy contributions to the study of international relations". The literature on autonomy by scholars such as Helio Jaguaribe and Juan Carlos Puig drew both on local ideas drawn from dependency theory and the UN Economic Commission on Latin America (ECLA) school as well as realism and interdependence (Tickner, 2014: 78). Different from how the term is used in mainstream theories as referring to a state's domestic capacities, in the Latin American reading, it implies "self-determination from other political entities, where protection against economic, political and cultural interference is sought for" (Miguez, 2021: 2). As a political concept, it has been seen "as an instrumental tool for safeguarding against the most noxious effects of the international system" and for safeguarding national sovereignty and development (Tickner, 2014: 82).[21] While recognising the value of the geocultural situatedness of knowing, and the importance of paying attention to context, there are also limitations to these approaches. For one, they tend to assume that there are entrenched differences between 'Europe' and the rest, but also amongst the rest, based on geocultural factors. The result is that they reflect the need to develop concepts and theories that are specific to understanding a particular place (and thereby arguably give credence to Eurocentric notions about the intrinsic particularity of knowledge emerging from the Global South. At the same time, they fail to consider the way in which geocultural situatedness is not independent of world politics nor the discipline of IR (refer to the discussion about worlding in Chapter 2).

Decentring

Related to the above concern that the Eurocentric bias inherent in existing FPA and foreign policy studies approaches makes them unsuitable for understanding foreign policy making in the Global South, some scholars have noted that Eurocentrism also poses a problem for the analysis of the foreign policies of European states and the EU. Specifically, they argue that in order to improve its relations with other states,

---

[21] For further detail on autonomy and Latin American IR, see Tickner (2003, 2009a, 2009b).

particularly in the Global South, the approaches applied should be decentred. Essentially, they interpret this as implying that the frameworks that work in understanding European foreign policy cannot be unquestioningly applied elsewhere, and that local context and alternative worldviews should be taken into account. In an attempt to "decentre" European foreign policy analysis, Stephan Keukeleire and Sharon Lecocq criticise the fact that a Eurocentric framing of history is often generalized to other parts of the world" (2018: 281). While their theoretical framework constitutes a potential challenge to FPA, empirically it falls short of providing new insights, and shares the same limitations of other decentring approaches outlined in Chapter 3. This includes a failure to rethink 'Europe' or how existing concepts and frameworks apply to it, as they only question their relevance in relation to other parts of the world. In addition, they also do not consider those outside 'Europe' as thinking actors who have been co-constitutive of the ideas, practices and institutions that are otherwise portrayed as having autonomously developed by 'Europe'.

Postcoloniality and Rewriting 'Commonsense' Narratives

One of the more explicit attempts at decolonising FPA is Mark Laffey and Jutta Weldes' "Decolonizing the Cuban Missile Crisis" (2008). In it, they emphasise how Cuba was written out of conventional IR accounts of the crisis, which focused on the Cold War competition between the superpowers. FPA analysts followed suit by focusing their attention on questions of foreign policy decision-making in the US, and making certain temporal and spatial assumptions about the beginning of the crisis that essentially erased the history of US imperialism. They argue that this is problematic in that it has had a troubling impact on IR theory and models of foreign policy decision-making (Laffey & Weldes, 2008: 556). In essence, the way in which the role of a subaltern state like Cuba was sidelined in knowledge practices reflects the lack of acknowledgement in both the practice of states and in academia of the role that these "lesser" states play in "making our world" (2008: 556). Laffey and Weldes convincingly show how "scholarly practices and the practices of states together produce a hierarchical international order in which Cuba is not a significant locus of agency or knowledge" (2008: 556). In other words, they challenge the selective narrative that suggests that explaining US foreign policy is the only story we need to know about the Cuban missile crisis. When the focus is shifted to Cuba, the Cuban missile crisis becomes less about a standoff between nuclear powers and deterrence than about "the sovereign rights of small states in a world dominated by great powers" (Laffey & Weldes, 2008: 566). The authors also show how Cuban articulations (that were heard during an oral history project on the crisis in the late 80s and early 90s) were translated into existing Eurocentric cognitive frames and framed as, for example, misperception (2008: 567). This underlines the notion that, even when it was included, the Cuban experience was misunderstood. This points to a failure to be puzzled that was also discussed in Chapter 3. Drawing on the revisionist tradition in US diplomatic history, they emphasise how "The global south becomes integral to how we conceive of the international. Attention shifts from the policies of great powers to the social relations through which they and other subjects of global life are connected, constituted, and produced." (2008: 571) Besides centring the agency of the Global South, the connectedness and co-constitution of different parts of the world and their foreign policies are foregrounded.

Going beyond the question of difference or similarity, Siba Grovogui problematises the way in which what constitutes understandings of foreign policy are themselves a product of Eurocentric assumptions about the nature of statehood and the international that have their origin in the colonial project. Criticising Western theorists for their inability to conceptualise foreign policy in a way "that might differ in both substance and ethos from that which emerged from modern Europe", he blames this on the fact that the study of international relations and foreign policy is based on ontological foundations that unquestioningly assume that postcolonial states will follow the same trajectory as Western states in their understandings of power, interests and values (2003: 31). Arguing that "in order to understand the historicity and peculiarity of the concept and practice of foreign policy, one must examine the historical conditions of the onto-logical coherence of the particular sets of human activities identified as foreign policy" (2003: 38), he identifies postcoloniality "as the basis of historical and spatial understandings of the purpose of foreign policy that differed markedly from its purpose in Europe and the West" (2003: 33). Together with other Postcolonial Studies scholars, he calls on us to take into account the enduring colonial legacies and their contemporary artic-ulations when trying to understand the foreign policies of states in the Global South.

Having considered some of the ways in which different scholars have tried to address US-centrism in FPA and the Eurocentrism in foreign policy studies, the next section presents an attempt at analysing foreign policy in a non-Eurocentric way. In an effort to move beyond the idea that Sinophone interpretations of relationality are particular to the Chinese context, what follows is an exploratory attempt to understand the foreign policy of a different state—South Africa—by drawing on elements of relational thinking advanced by Chinese scholars.

A RELATIONAL APPROACH TO SOUTH AFRICA'S FOREIGN POLICY

As discussed in Chapter 3, relationality includes a wide variety of approaches that claim to take a relational approach to studying the world. The aim here is not to provide an overview of what relational approaches to IR entail—others[22] have already done this, but some clarification is in order. While there are variations in different relational approaches, for example with regard to the extent to which they challenge anthropocentrism, their main commonality is that they regard relations as being ontologically prior to actors, in other words, the social world is one based on relations rather than separation. In addition, the identities of social actors are shaped through the process of relating. It follows that "[t]here is no isolated self, but only self-in-relations; and there is no self-interest defined in isolation, but only self-interest defined in relation to other-interest" (Qin, 2020: 170). This means that foreign policy is then not an outcome of state action but rather of a process of interaction.

The area of study in which we have seen relationality applied most prominently is China's foreign policy.[23] At the same time, there has been much criticism of the way in which some Chinese scholars have employed relationality to emphasise China's difference and reproduce the same binaries that they accuse 'Western IR' of.[24] Whilst recognising these critiques, I still see tremendous potential in applying a relational approach

---

[22] See Kavalski (2023) and Kurki (2019, 2022). Also see Chapter 3.

[23] Kavalski (2016) and Liu et al. (2022) provide a review of some of the work on China that takes a relational approach, outlining the differences between them. For further examples, see Song (2020), Shih (2019), Pan (2018).

[24] See Kavalski (2023), Shih (2022).

as a way to open up new avenues for studying and making sense of foreign policy.

It has become common practice for analysts and commentators to describe South Africa's post-apartheid foreign policy as ambiguous or inconsistent, due to the tendency to act in ways that seem to undermine its national interests and values. However, taking into account the criticism of scholars like Grovogui (2003) mentioned above, one has to ask which understanding of the national interest these critics hold, and whether they base their understandings on an individualist-rationalist framework. Attempts to explain this apparent inconsistency have ranged from an emphasis on of a clear foreign policy strategy to interpretations focused on the state's (multiple) identities.[25] As mentioned in Chapter 3, in encountering phenomena that seem to defy 'commonsense' explanations, it is important to be puzzled, and to search for alternative ways of explication.

Putting aside materialist explanations and instead staying within the realm of identity and relations, while the analyses focusing on multiple identities and role theory have been fruitful, they remain wedded to an individualist ontology in which the South African state exists as a social actor prior to interaction, and has multiple identities which it can choose to prioritise in any given situation. The major difference between the way in which role theory conceives of identity versus the way in which it is conceived in relational approaches is that in the former identity (or rather multiple identities) of actors already exist prior to interaction while according to the latter, identities are created through interaction, or relations. In other words, a role theory approach might suggest that South Africa has multiple predetermined identities, of which liberal democracy, developing state, African regional power, and anti-imperial power might be some. Depending on the context and which actor it is relating to, it might choose to perform or project one or more of these identities.

From a relational perspective, however, there are no pre-existing identities, and the actors themselves are not separate but rather constituted through interaction and the process of relations. It follows then that identities (and by association interests) do not exist prior to relations. While scholars such as Nizar Messari (2001), Lene Hansen (2006) and David Campbell (1998) also see foreign policy as being essential to the

---

[25] See, for example, Nathan (2005), Serrao and Bischoff (2009), Naidu (2015)

constitution and production of the state's identity, they tend to ascribe more agency to the state as a force that, through its foreign policy, both produces its own identities and those of other states. Their approaches are also based on a clear distinction between self and other, grounded in the idea that identity results from a continuous production of otherness.

While, as noted in the previous section, there are many different relational approaches, I draw on Qin's idea of 'relational identity' whereby identities and roles are shaped by social relations, allowing states to have multiple identities resulting from 'overlapping relational circles of various types and with different natures' (2018:132). I also employ Qin (2016: 37) and Qin and Nordin's (2019: 607) notion of the 'relational circle,' which is a key concept in Confucian relationality. According to this view, the actor is at the centre of concentric relationship circles extending outward from the self, with proximity to the self indicating greater intimacy. Relatedly, they hold that the more intimate a relational circle is, the more influential it is on the identity of the actor (2019: 608). Similarly, in previous work (Smith 2012) I employed the metaphor of the African family and community structure to show how South Africa's relational circles start with neighbouring African states that can be regarded as part of the clan (i.e. kinship group or the extended family, with members showing support towards and solidarity with one another); then proceeds to other African states who might be regarded as part of the tribe (where the relationship is not as close as with clan members, but still based on feelings of solidarity and shared values); and the rest of the developing world as neighbouring, and mostly friendly tribes. The Global North is situated in the outermost, and thus least intimate circle. This is reflected in South Africa's foreign policy white paper, which states that South Africa 'accords central importance to our immediate African neighbourhood and continent; working with countries of the South to address shared challenges of underdevelopment; promoting global equity and social justice; working with countries of the North to develop a true and effective partnership for a better world' (DIRCO, 2016: 4).

A question that remains, however, is why relations matter most to particular states. In other words, relationality becomes essential to understanding why certain relations are more important in shaping an actor's identity and its interests. While Qin and Nordin contend that the more intimate a relationship is (those in the innermost circle), the more influence it has on the actor's decisions and actions (2019: 608), they do not elaborate on what the basis for intimacy is. Is it the thickness of existing relations? And is this based on the regularity of interaction, or on other factors such as geographical proximity, shared history, shared culture, shared worldview? This is an area that thus requires further exploration, and where the case of South Africa might be able to provide us with insights that could be more widely applicable to thinking about relationality. How do relationships come about, how do they create or shape actors, and why are some stronger or more intimate than others? Qin (2018), for example, views relations as natural occurrences, including the positional power inherent in these relationships. An alternative understanding is that relationships are shaped by factors such as shared experiences and histories (e.g. of colonialism), by geo-cultural proximity and similarities (which could include linguistic and other cultural features), or that regular interaction results in thicker, more intimate relations. In the South African case, the history of the relationship between the current South African state and its counterparts is particularly important. For example, historical instances of loyalty and solidarity seem to bear more weight than other more obvious considerations (based on existing foreign policy frameworks) such as material interest. The South African government's support of Russia despite its invasion of Ukraine is a case in point. In an attempt to explain the South African position, the Soviet Union's support for the liberation struggle against apartheid, when the West (in particular the USA and the UK) were supportive of the apartheid government, is frequently cited. Elaborating on this point in a much more sophisticated manner, Naude (2022) suggests that the South African state's behaviour can be understood by foregrounding the role of past experiences of the state's relations with Others.

In my attempt to think globally about South Africa's foreign policy, my contention is that foreign policy actions that flow from relations can in turn strengthen or reify particular identities. In this way, the foreign policy process is itself constitutive of identities, in an endless loop between relations and identities. The actor (in this case the South African state) interprets certain relations and the identities that emerge from them as more significant and acts in ways that re-inscribe particular identities. To this extent, thus, actors both have agency, and are shaped by relations. While the identities that shape relations can become entrenched and even naturalised over time, they are also often deliberately enacted by state actors. Insights from the literature on friendship (a special type of relationship) in IR are also relevant here. Felix Berenskoetter (2007), for example, has contended that while geographical proximity, shared culture of political system, trade, shared membership of institutions, and so forth are important criteria for friendship (which is a form of intimate relationship) they are not sufficient. Instead, he argued that "friendship designates an intimate relationship between states voluntarily bonded by a shared moral space (sense of virtue) grown out of significant experiences and translated into a genuine commitment to a common project which lends significance to the future." In short, friendship, as an evolving relationship, is a process of building a 'common world' to which states become emotionally attached (Berenskoetter, 2007:670). For example, while South Africa's geographical position naturally implies that it is an African state, the identity of African-ness (and what the different assumptions and expectations underlying this designator) especially with regards to foreign policy behaviour is one that is learned and performed. For example, despite its geographical positioning, the South African state under apartheid was very much *not* an African state – both in the way the state enacted its own identity and also how it was perceived by other African states. Being part of the intimate relational group of 'African states' is therefore not automatic (as, for example, Morocco has also experienced) and the relationships must be both actively pursued by the state in question, and be supported and cultivated by others in the group – particularly powerful[26] members. Not all African states have equal influence in this regard, and sub-regional and regional power dynamics are significant determinants.

Drawing on the idea of the South African state's relational circles, one could contend that while the relations that are deemed to be most important are those within the most intimate relational circles, namely (southern) African neighbours, South Africa is simultaneously engaged in multiple other relations that also constitute different identities. These include the Global South and anti-Western/anti-imperial identity cultivated through relations with partners in the Non-Aligned Movement[27] and G77, individual states with which it has intimate historical relations like Russia, China and Cuba, as well as relations with 'the West' that constitute it as a regional leader, a liberal democracy and maintainer of continental peace and stability. South Africa's efforts to maintain these

---

[26] The type of power referred to here could be material, institutional or ideational.

[27] While South Africa only joined the NAM in 1994 after its first democratic election, the movement was instrumental in galvanising international solidarity against the apartheid regime, and South Africa has been an active member.

different relations and accompanying identities has resulted in sometimes surprising and inexplicable foreign policy actions and decisions which, in turn, has resulted in criticisms of an inconsistent and ambiguous foreign policy. For example, its quest to solidify its identity as an African state that prioritises the interests of the continent in its foreign policy have frequently clashed with its identity as a liberal democracy with a value-driven foreign policy. Inevitably, relations overlap and come into conflict with one another. This has manifested in a number of specific foreign policy actions, including South Africa's refusal to arrest Sudanese President al-Bashir under the ICC warrant, and numerous votes in the UN Security Council and the Human Rights Council (HRC) that were heavily criticised by Western powers and potentially damaging to South Africa's relations with these states (from a perspective that views national interest as primarily materialist and individualist). One specific issue relates to South Africa's stance on the promotion of sexual orientation and gender identity (SOGI) rights in the UN.[28] Once regarded as a role model for human rights on the African continent, it was the first country to enshrine LGBT+ rights in its constitution. Internationally, South Africa took the lead in calling for global acceptance of LGBT+ rights, and in 2011, its leadership was considered critical to pass a HRC resolution to recognise these rights as human rights. In July 2016, however, in a vote that surprised many, the South African delegation abstained on a key vote in the HRC to appoint an independent watchdog on sexual orientation. This was in line with the position of other African states, not one of whom voted in favour of the resolution. In cases like this, South Africa often justifies its positions on the basis that it must show solidarity with the rest of Africa. In other words, its relations with its most intimate circle become the overriding consideration, and trumps relations with the USA and Europe, as a state that supports progressive liberal human rights and upholds the agreed-to rules of the multilateral system. While some commentators might regard such action as inconsistent or even irrational, the logic of relationality holds that 'an actor's individualistic rationality is necessarily mediated by his or her relationships with others' (Qin & Nordin, 2019: 609).

    In conclusion, this section has attempted to apply the idea of relational circles to understanding South Africa's foreign policy making, and also

---

[28] See Jordaan (2020, 2017) and Berry (2021) for further detail.

to draw out further questions and insights raised by this case. Essentially, foreign policy behaviour is influenced by the existing relationship to a given actor/set of actors. By emphasising the importance of different relations in South Africa's foreign policy, we can therefore understand, as Shih and Huang (2015: 3) argue that, starting from the position of relationality, what comes across as double standards or inconsistency in foreign policy is in fact a 'systemic necessity', but according to a different understanding of the system, rather than a form of idiosyncrasy. One possible answer to the puzzle of why SA takes foreign policy decisions that do not seem to make sense (or do not seems rational) from the perspective of individual interest-based calculations is therefore that it attaches more value to relations that are the result of thicker forms of interaction, based for example on shared traumatic experiences like colonialism.

Conclusion

Starting from the assumption that the study of foreign policy, as one of the main areas of interest of IR scholars, suffers from a similar affliction of Eurocentrism as the field of IR in general, this chapter has attempted to provide a brief overview of existing attempts at studying foreign policy in a more global manner. The various approaches can be said to diverge on the basis of how they think about and deal with assumed differences based on geocultural situatedness. If certain states are believed to be essentially different from others, this might result in approaches that highlight the need for alternative theoretical and analytical frameworks. If, on the other hand, the way in which foreign policy (regardless of the context) has been studied is deemed problematic due to the ontological assumptions underlying the entire endeavour, then a more far-reaching rethinking of assumptions about individualist-rationalist action may be the solution. Relational approaches provide potential to think foreign policy globally, and to avoid the trap of further essentialising difference. As noted throughout, the positions of different scholars—including this author's—on these questions has evolved over time, and the aim here is not to prescribe 'the right way' to think globally about foreign policy, but to continue to be puzzled and to experiment with different approaches. Having said that, it is also important to note that some are more limited in terms of their potential for doing this in a way that does not simply entrench Eurocentric binaries, adopt an 'add and stir' strategy or try to pluralise without taking into account the structural impediments related to historical and contemporary power dynamics and the politics of knowledge.

Bibliography

Adar, K. G. (2015). Foreign Policy Processes in African States. In K. Brummer & V. M. Hudson (Eds.), *Foreign Policy Analysis Beyond North America* (pp. 101–119). Lynne Rienner.

Adar, K. G., & Ajulu, R. (Eds.). (2002). *Globalization and Emerging Trends in African States' Foreign Policy-Making Process: A Comparative Perspective of Southern Africa*. Ashgate.

Adar, K. G., & Schraeder, P. J. (Eds.) (2007). *Globalization and Emerging Trends in African Foreign Policy, Vol II: A Comparative Perspective of Eastern Africa*. Africa Institute of South Africa and University Press of America.

Alden, C. and Aran, A. (2012). *Foreign Policy Analysis: New Approaches*. Routledge.

Ayoob, M.H. (2002). Inequality and Theorizing in International Relations: The Case for Subaltern Realism. *International Studies Review*, 4, 27–48.

Bell, D. A. (2017). Realizing Tianxia: Traditional Values and China's Foreign Policy. In B. Wang (Ed.), *Chinese Visions of World Order: Tianxia, Culture, and World Politics* (pp. 129–146). Duke University Press.

Berenskoetter, F. (2007). Friends, There are no Friends? An Intimate Reframing of the International. *Millennium, 35*(3), 647–676.

Berry, N. (2021). *Queering South Africa's International Promulgation of SOGI Rights* (Unpublished PhD dissertation). University of Cape Town.

Braveboy-Wagner, J. A. (Ed.). (2003). *The Foreign Policies of the Global South: Rethinking Conceptual Frameworks*. Lynne Rienner.

Brummer, K. (2015). Implications for Mainstream FPA Theory. In K. Brummer & V. M. Hudson (Eds.), *Foreign Policy Analysis Beyond North America* (pp. 169–186). Lynne Rienner.

Brummer, K. (2021). Advancing Foreign Policy Analysis by Studying Leaders from the Global South. *International Affairs, 97*(2), 405–421.

Brummer, K., & Hudson, V. M. (Eds.) (2015). *Foreign Policy Analysis Beyond North America*. Lynne Rienner.

Brummer, K., & Hudson, V. M. (2017). The Boundedness of Foreign Policy Analysis Theory? *Global Society, 31*(2), 157–166.

Çalkivik, A. (2020). Foreign Policy. In A.B. Tickner & K. Smith (Eds.). (2020). *International Relations from the Global South: Worlds of Difference (1st ed.)*. Routledge.

Callahan, W.A. (2008). Chinese Visions of World Order: Post-hegemonic or a New Hegemony?, *International Studies Review, 10*(4), 749–761.

Campbell, D. (1998). *Writing Security: United States Foreign Policy and the Politics of Identity*. University of Minnesota.

Chabal, P., & Daloz, J. P. (2006). *Culture Troubles: Politics and the Interpretation of Meaning*. Hurst.

Clapham, C. (1977). *Foreign Policy Making in Developing States: A Comparative Approach*. Saxon House.

Clark, J. F. (2001). Foreign Policy Making in Central Africa: The New Imperative of Regime Security in a New Context. In G. Khadiagala & T. Lyons (Eds.), *African Foreign Policies: Power and Process* (pp. 67–86). Lynne Rienner.

De Coning, C., Mandrup, T., & Odgaard, L. (Eds.). (2015). *The BRICS and Coexistence: An Alternative Vision of World Order*. Routledge.

Escudé, C. (1998)."An Introduction to Peripheral Realism". In S.G. Neuman (Ed.). *International Relations Theory and the Third World*. (pp. 55–75). St. Martin's Press.

Fortin, C., Heine, J., & Ominami, C. (Eds.). (2023). *Latin American Foreign Policies in the New World Order: The Active Non-Alignment Option*. Anthem Press.

Ganguly, S., & Pardesi, M. J. (2015). Foreign Policy Analysis in India. In K. Brummer & V. M. Hudson (Eds.), *Foreign Policy Analysis Beyond North America* (pp. 57–76). Lynne Rienner.

Giacolone, R. (2015). Latin American Foreign Policy Analysis. In K. Brummer & V. M. Hudson (Eds.), *Foreign Policy Analysis Beyond North America*. Lynne Rienner.

Grovogui, S. (2003). Postcoloniality in Global South Foreign Policy: A Perspective. In J. A. Braveboy-Wagner (Ed.), *The Foreign Policies of the Global South: Rethinking Conceptual Frameworks*. Lynne Rienner.

Hansen, L. (2006). *Security as Practice: Discourse Analysis and the Bosnian War*. Francis & Taylor.

Herborth, B. (2015). Do We Need 195 Theories of Foreign Policy? In G. Hellman and K.E. Jorgensen (Eds.). *Theorizing Foreign Policy in a Globalized World*. (pp. 101–125), Palgrave Macmillan.

Hellman, G., & Jorgensen, K. E. (Eds.). (2015). *Theorizing Foreign Policy in a Globalized World*. Palgrave Macmillan.

Hinnebusch, R., & Ehteshami, A. (Eds.). (2014). *The Foreign Policies of Middle Eastern States* (2nd ed.). Lynne Rienner.

Hinnebusch, R. (2015). Foreign Policy Analysis and the Arab World. In K. Brummer & V. M. Hudson (Eds.), *Foreign Policy Analysis Beyond North America* (pp. 77–99). Lynne Rienner.

Hoffman, S. (1977). An American Social Science: International Relations. *Daedalus, 106*(3), 41–60.

Hudson, V. M. (2015). Foreign Policy Analysis Beyond North America. In K. Brummer & V. M. Hudson (Eds.), *Foreign Policy Analysis Beyond North America* (pp. 1–13). Lynne Rienner.

Jordaan, E. (2003). The concept of a middle power in international relations: distinguishing between emerging and traditional middle powers. *Politikon, 30*(1), 165–181.

Jordaan, E. (2020). *South Africa and the UN Human Rights Council: The Fate of the Liberal Order*. Routledge.

Jordaan, E. (2017). South Africa and Sexual Orientation Rights at the United Nations: Batting for Both Sides. *Politikon, 44*(2), 205–230.

Kavalski, E. (2016). Review: Relationality and Its Chinese Characteristics, *The China Quarterly*, 226 (June), 551–559.

Kavalski, E. (2023). 'Relational Theories in International Relations'. *Oxford Research Encyclopedia of International Studies*. Retrieved 9 December 2023, from https://oxfordre.com/internationalstudies/view/10.1093/acrefore/9780190846626.001.0001/acrefore-9780190846626-e-681

Keukeleire, S., & Lecocq, S. (2018). Operationalising the Decentring Agenda: Analysing European Foreign Policy in a Non-European and Post-western World. *Cooperation and Conflict, 53*(2), 277–295.

Khadiagala, G., & Lyons, T. (2001). Foreign Policy Making in Africa: An Introduction. In G. Khadiagala & T. Lyons (Eds.), *African Foreign Policies: Power and Process* (pp. 1–13). Lynne Rienner.

Korany, B. (1986). *How Foreign Policy Decisions are Made in the Third World: A Comparative Analysis*. Routledge.

Korany, B., & Hillal Desouki, A. E. (Eds.). (2008). *The Foreign Policies of Arab States: The Challenges of Globalization* (3rd ed.). American University of Cairo Press.

Kurki, M. (2022). Relational Revolution and Relationality in IR: New Conversations. *Review of International Studies, 48*(5), 821–836.

Kurki, M. (2019). Critical theory, relational thought and relational cosmology. *Routledge Handbook of Critical International Relations*. London and New York: Routledge.

Laffey, M. & Weldes, J. (2008). Decolonizing the Cuban Missile Crisis, *International Studies Quarterly, 52*(3), 555–577.

Liu, S., Garlick, J., & Qin, F. (2022). Towards Guanxi? Reconciling the 'Relational Turn' in Western and Chinese International Relations Scholarship. *All Azimuth, 11*(1), 67–85.

Messari, N. (2001). Identity and Foreign Policy – The Case of Islam in US Foreign Policy. In V. Kubalkova (Ed.). *Foreign Policy in a Constructed World* (pp. 227–248). ME Sharpe.

Miguez, M. C. (2021). Autonomy in Foreign Policy: A Latin American Contribution to International Relations Theory. In *Oxford Research Encyclopedia of International Studies.* https://oxfordre.com/internationalstudies/view/ 10.1093/acrefore/9780190846626.001.0001/acrefore-9780190846626- e-647, accessed 2 June 2023.

Ministry of External Affairs of India (MEA) (n.d.) *Panchsheel.* Available at https://www.mea.gov.in/Uploads/PublicationDocs/191_panchsheel.pdf, accessed 15 July 2023.

Naidu, S. (2015). Understanding South Africa's Global Governance Identity. In L. Masters, S. Zondi, J. A. van Wyk, & C. Landsberg (Eds.), *South African Foreign Policy Review: Volume 2* (pp. 59–72). AISA.

Nathan, L. (2005). Consistency and Inconsistencies in South African Foreign Policy. *International Affairs, 81*(2), 361–372.

Naude, B. (2022). *Revisiting State Personhood and World Politics: Identity, Personality and the IR Subject.* Routledge.

Pan, C. (2018). Towards a New Relational Ontology in Global Politics: China's Rise as Haolographic Transition. *International Relations of the Asia-Pacific, 18*(3), 339–367.

Qin, Y. (2016). A Relational Theory of World Politics. *International Studies Review, 18,* 33–47.

Qin, Y. (2018). *A Relational Theory of World Politics.* Cambridge University Press.

Qin, Y., & Nordin, A. (2019). Relationality and rationality in Confucian and Western traditions. *Cambridge Review of International Affairs, 32*(5), 601– 614.

Qin, Y. (2020). Diplomacy as Relational Practice. *The Hague Journal of Diplomacy, 15*(1–2), 165–173.

Schoeman, M. (2000). South Africa as an emerging middle power. *African Security Review, 9*(3), 47–58.

Schenoni, L., & Escude, C. (2016). Peripheral Realism Revisited. *Revista Brasileira de Politica Internacional, 59*(1), 1–18.

Serrao, O., & Bischoff, P. H. (2009). Foreign Policy Ambiguity on the Part of an Emerging Middle Power: South African Foreign Policy Through Other Lenses. *South African Journal of International Affairs, 36*(3), 363–380.

Shih, C-Y. & Huang, C-C. (2015). China's Quest for Grand Strategy: Power, National Interest, or Relational Security?, *The Chinese Journal of International Politics, 8*(1), 1–26.

Shih, C.-Y. (2019). *China and International Theory: The Balance of Relation- ships.* Routledge.

Shih, C.-Y. (2022). *Post-Chineseness.* State University of New York Press.

Smith, K. (2012). Contrived Boundaries, Kinship and Ubuntu: A (South) African View of the International. In A. Tickner & D. Blaney (Eds.), *Thinking International Relations Differently.* Routledge.

Smith, S., Hadfield, A., & Dunne, T. (Eds.) (2016). *Foreign Policy: Theories, Actors, Cases* (3rd ed.). Oxford University Press.

Smith, K. (2018). Reshaping International Relations: Innovations from Africa. *All Azimuth: A Journal of Foreign Policy and Peace,* 7(2), 81–92.

Song, W. (2020). China's Normative Foreign Policy and Its Multilateral Engagement in Asia. *Pacific Focus: Inha Journal of International Studies, XXXXV* (2), 229–249.

Tickner, A. (2003). Hearing Latin American Voices in IR. *International Studies Perspectives,* 4(4), 325–350.

Tickner, A. (2009). Latin American IR and the Primary of lo práctico. *International Studies Review,* 10(4), 735–748.

Tickner, A. B. (2009b). Latin America. Still Policy Dependent after All These Years? In A. B. Tickner & O. Waever (Eds.), *International Relations Scholarship around the World* (pp. 32–52). Routledge.

Tickner, A. B. (2014). Autonomy and Latin American International Relations Thinking. In J. Dominguez & A. Covarrubias (Eds.), *Routledge Handbook of Latin America in the World* (pp. 74–84). Routledge.

Zhao, T. (2009). A political world. *Diogenes,* 56(5), 5–18.

Zhao, T. (2021). *All under heaven: The tianxia system for a possible world order.* University of California Press.

Conclusion

Pinar Bilgin and Karen Smith

Abstract Chapter 6 highlights one issue that the book has not addressed, namely the structural barriers to thinking globally about world politics. In particular, it emphasises the issue of English as the hegemonic language of IR and also the Anglo-Saxon intellectual style. Without dismissing the constraints inhibiting non-English speakers or those not sufficiently proficient in English or the Anglo-Saxon style to publish in English-speaking outlets, we note another issue. This is the marginalisation experienced by those who do write and publish in English but whose work is not read by their peers for a variety of reasons. Regarding the latter, the chapter asks whether this represents an often overlooked problem, namely the failure of IR scholars to engage with fellow scholars as coeval thinkers—even as they write and publish in English.

Keywords Language · English · Anglo-Saxon intellectual style · Coeval

Our starting point in the book was the observation that a wealth of information is available regarding centuries of mutual interaction and learning between the world's peoples across space and time. However, our field of IR continues to draw from the same historical narratives when formulating its concepts and theories. We also observed that even when those interactions are acknowledged, very little of it is brought to

P. Bilgin and K. Smith, *Thinking Globally About World Politics: Beyond Global IR*, https://doi.org/10.1007/978-3-031-56572-4_6

133

bear on IR concepts and theories. Consider how quickly the 'Global IR and Regional Worlds' agenda of ISA 2015 has bifurcated into critiques of the global/globality in IR theorising on the one hand, and exploration of regions on the other, with little conversation between these two bodies of scholarship. It is against this background that we decided to write this book.

Both of us have been engaged in efforts to address IR's Eurocentric limitations since the early 2000s. In the Postscript, together with others, we reflect on our own trials and travails. While it is twenty years for the two of us, the broader body of effort has a much longer history. In the book, we orientate ourselves not to the current debates on the so-called 'globalising turn', but go to the heart of the matter at hand, addressing IR's Eurocentric limitations. In doing so, we built upon the critiques advanced by postcolonial, feminist and decolonising approaches and insisted that the question is not "why is there no non-Western IR theory?" (as originally asked by Acharya and Buzan in 2007), but rather: Why is it that scholars of IR do not pay attention to the wealth of knowledge already available when addressing the Eurocentric limitations of their concepts and theories? Why do we not read and learn from what is out there?

We can imagine some IR scholars being offended by this question. It is in our job description as scholars to read, and we read a lot. But, what do we read? Do we go beyond the known outlets? Do we engage with scholars from other parts of the world as our coevals who also think and write about world politics? Eurocentrism circumscribes our understanding of the international not because other parts of the world are missing, but because they are incorporated in a very particular way that overlooks the latter's contributions. Such contributions go back centuries, but are also happening as we write.

As we stressed throughout the book, the solution is not 'adding' what is presumed to be 'absent'. It is the very presumption of 'absence' that needs addressing head on, because such presumptions are the bedrock of Eurocentrism. Put differently, Eurocentrism persists notwithstanding all our efforts, because we have so far focused on the normative and analytical dimensions, missing the epistemological ones. Our own approach, thinking globally about world politics, involves curiosity about what others think about the world, making a sustained effort to locate the knowledge they have produced, and recognising their contributions (past and present) to what we otherwise view as 'European' ideas, practices, and institutions.

One issue that we have not addressed in the book is the structural barriers to the kind of effort that we envision. What about those who cannot or do not want to write in English, or publish, or disseminate their publications? How do we access their thoughts? Is this not an insurmountable problem for thinking globally about world politics? Indeed, there are scholars working in IR in the non-English speaking world and the wider Global South whose work is not familiar to us. We do not know what we are missing; that is true. But we did not let this paralyse us; instead, we worked through this paradox (as with some others), in the spirit of both/and.

While language is a part of the problem here (see below), there is also the issue of intellectual style. Over the years, the "Anglo-Saxon intellectual style, with brief, straightforward statements and linear progression of an argument" has frustrated non-English speakers due to acting as a barrier to "expressing real complexity" (Waever, 1998: 694). In addition, it has also come to be confused with a 'proper scholarly' style of writing. The result is that the work of those who do not write in this style are often deemed less-than-scholarly and oftentimes desk-rejected by journal and book editors. Indeed, for those seeking to get published in the familiar outlets of IR, the issue is not merely command over the English language but command of this style. While there are alternative publishing outlets, due to the power dynamics in global knowledge dissemination, including publishing, the alternatives do not have the same reach. As a result of adopting this style, some scholars worry about how it impacts on how they write and construct arguments, to the extent that it may result in a (subconscious) reflection of Anglophone history and culture. In the words of Kosuke Shimizu (2014: 86), "To understand IR, we naturally feel the need to internalise not only the language structure but also its historical and cultural background."

On the issue of language, as with the debates on 'Master's tools' (see Chapter 3), the question of the English language is even more complex than initially meets the eye. Keeping with the book's both/and spirit, the dominance of English in IR is both a problem and not a problem. It is a problem for the aforementioned reasons, which cannot be overlooked. Yet it is not a problem at the same time, and this book itself is a testament to that. We were able to write a book such as this by relying mostly on English-language resources. We do not know what else we could have accessed if we looked beyond the five languages that we know between the two of us. But then, we relied on the English-language scholarship of authors who do have access to their own geocultural resources, who reflect on their settings, and produce knowledge. This does not mean that we dismiss the constraints inhibiting non-English speakers or those not sufficiently proficient in English to publish in English-speaking outlets. This remains an impediment, and there are undoubtedly valuable insights that have remained hidden from the wider IR readership. But there are many others who do publish in English and whose work is accessible. The question is whether we engage with them as coeval thinkers.

Finally, whilst we appreciate the significance of the debates about writing in a colonial language in a postcolonial context, we agree with those who contend that English is no longer only the language of the United Kingdom or the United States, and in that sense, language may have been separated or freed from a particular cultural context. Indeed, there are multiple Englishes (Shimizu, 2014), and the English language now has a wide variety of global consumers and co-producers who have not only adopted and adapted it for their own purposes, but who co-constitute it in the same way we have argued that 'knowledge' about world politics associated with 'Europe' has been co-constituted.

In conclusion, we hope to have answered some of your questions about how to think globally about world politics, although the aim was not to provide a comprehensive 'how to' guide. At the same time, we hope that new questions have been raised as a result. In particular, we hope that you are puzzled anew about your research, perhaps in ways that you were not before. As emphasised throughout, embracing discomfort, and continuing to be puzzled about the world are prerequisites for thinking globally about world politics.

BIBLIOGRAPHY

Shimizu, K. (2014). Who Owns Our Tongue? English, Academic Life, and Subjectivity. In K. Shimizu & W.S. Bradley (Eds.) *Multiculturalism and Conflict Reconciliation in the Asia-Pacific: Migration, Language, and Politics* (pp. 81–98). Palgave MacMillan.

Waever, O. (1998). The Sociology of a Not So International Discipline: American and European Developments in International Relations. *International Organization, 52*(4), 687–727.

Postscript: Getting Lost, Feeling Puzzled

Karen Smith

Introduction

As discussed throughout the book, the recent 'globalising turn' builds on decades of groundwork that was done by a range of scholars, some of whom are sometimes referred to while others are never or rarely cited in more recent work. I found it important to highlight the insights of some of these scholars regarding what drove them to pursue these issues, who and what influenced their thinking, and where they think the debate is and should be going. Engaging with individual scholars emphasises positionality, whilst recognising that it is not the only thing that matters. As Pinar Bilgin says in her interview, positionality informs rather than defines. It is however important in terms of understanding the different positions individuals have taken in the debate about how to go about the project of addressing Eurocentrism in IR. As we point out in Chapter 3, scholars' backgrounds and experiences influence the questions they ask, the approaches they prefer, and the methods they choose.

P. Bilgin and K. Smith, *Thinking Globally About World Politics: Beyond Global IR*, https://doi.org/10.1007/978-3-031-56572-4

By focusing on a handful of scholars in this chapter, I leave out many who have played a crucial role in helping us to think globally about world politics. Instead, the choice is an unashamedly personal one: I highlight those whose work influenced me when I first became interested in the topic of how IR (theory) relates to the Global South in the early 2000s. This chapter is therefore the outcome of my own early reading list, which has subsequently expanded to include the authors mentioned in previous chapters, and many others who have since joined the ranks of those criticising (for there are indeed many) and offering solutions (there are far fewer) to the problem of Eurocentrism in IR. Besides Arlene Tickner's 2003 article "Postcards from the Third World", one of the earliest sources I came across was Stephanie Neuman's[1] edited 1998 volume *International Relations Theory and the Third World*. Conceived while she was teaching a course on Third World Security at Columbia University in the 1990s, the book asked whether Western International Relations theory is relevant for understanding what we now refer to as the Global South. Noting how central concepts such as anarchy, sovereignty and the state "have little apparent reference to objective reality and evidence a normative stance in which Western ideas and institutions are not only considered to be universal but, implicitly, also superior" (Neuman, 1998: 2) the volume included contributions from authors such as Amitav Acharya, Barry Buzan, Mohammed Ayoob, Donald Puchala, and Carlos Escude, who not only outlined the shortcomings of existing theory but also presented alternative explanations. Soon after, I discovered Kevin Dunn and Tim Shaw's edited volume *Africa's Challenge to International Relations*, which took a similar approach to Neuman's book, but with a focus on the African continent.

This chapter draws on exchanges I have had with different scholars over the years, but specifically on in-depth conversations[2] with Pinar

---

[1] Unfortunately Stephanie Neuman passed away in 2020 and I was never able to meet or speak to her.

[2] Interview with Pinar Bilgin. Conducted by Karen Smith, 23 June 2022; Interview with Kevin Dunn. Conducted by Karen Smith, 23 August 2023 (online); Interview with Siddharth Mallavarapu. Conducted by Karen Smith, 28 August 2023 (online); Interview with Arlene Tickner. Conducted by Karen Smith, 2 November 2023 (online).

Bilgin,[3] Arlene Ticker,[4] Kevin Dunn,[5] and Siddharth Mallavarapu.[6] Except where indicated otherwise, quotes are from these conversations and have been edited lightly for clarity.

LOOKING IN FROM THE MARGINS

One question I was interested in finding answers to is what drew these scholars to thinking about the problem of Eurocentrism in IR in the first place. While the issue has received more attention in recent years, which has resulted in greater awareness and interest amongst a wider range of scholars, this was not always the case. Twenty years ago the group of people working on this topic was still very small indeed, and relegated to the fringes of conferences like the International Studies Association (ISA) conventions. I was curious whether individual scholars' backgrounds had something to do with it, whether there was a particular incident that triggered their interest, or specific influences in the form of people or literature, for example.

[3] Key publications include: Bilgin, P. (2008). Thinking Past 'Western' IR? *Third World Quarterly, 29*(1), 5-23; Bilgin, P. (2016). Edward Said's 'contrapuntal reading' as a method, an ethos and a metaphor for Global IR. *International Studies Review*, 18(1), 134-146; Bilgin, P. (2016). Do IR scholars engage with the same world? In K. Booth & T. Erskine (Eds.), *International Relations Theory Today* (2nd. ed.): Polity; Bilgin, P. (2016). *The International in Security, Security in the International*. London: Routledge.

[4] Key publications: Tickner, A. (2003). Seeing IR differently: notes from the Third World. *Millennium-Journal of International Studies, 32*(2), 295-324; Tickner, A. B. and Blaney, D. (Eds.). (2012). *Thinking International Relations Differently* (Vol. 2). London: Routledge; Tickner, A. B., & Smith, K. (2020). *International Relations from the Global South: Worlds of Difference*: Routledge; Tickner, A. B., and Waever, O. (Eds.). (2009). *International Relations Scholarship Around the World*. London: Routledge.

[5] Key publications include: Dunn, K. (2003). *Imagining the Congo: The International Relations of Identity*. Houndsmills: Palgrave Macmillan; Dunn, K. (2020). *Global Punk: Resistance and Rebellion in Everyday Life*. London: Bloomsbury Academic. 2016; Dunn, K. and Englebert, P. (2020) *Inside African Politics. 2nd Edition*. Boulder: Lynne Rienner Press.

[6] Key publications include: Mallavarapu, S. (2018). The Sociology of International Relations in India: Competing Conceptions of Political Order. In Hellmann, G. (Ed.) *Theorizing Global Order* (pp.142-171), Frankfurt and New York: Campus Verlag; Chimni, B.S. and Mallavarapu, S. (Eds.) (2012). *International Relations: Perspectives for the Global South*. New Delhi: Pearson; Bajpai, K.P. and Mallavarapu, S. (Eds.) (2005) *International Theory in India: Bringing Theory Back Home*. New Delhi: Orient Longman.

Arlene Tickner knows exactly when she experienced her moment of unease that served as the catalyst for her groundbreaking work in what was first described as non-Western IR, a term she herself now prefers not to use. It was in the 1990s, when she arrived in Colombia from the US and was asked to teach an Introduction to IR course, which included a theoretical component that she knew nothing about. Having to educate herself through the classical IR theory reading suggested by colleagues, she soon felt a tremendous sense of discomfort as a US-born, untrained (in IR) scholar "repeating quite mechanically, the teachings of the likes of Morgenthau, Waltz, Keohane and Nye in a classroom in Colombia", without any reflection on the way in which international relations was studied and foreign policy was thought about there. This led her to pursuing a PhD on the topic of intellectual hegemony in the field, in which she conducted a state of the art of IR in Latin America. She notes how, at the time, there was very little literature in IR on this topic, with Ole Waever's 1998 article "The Sociology of a Not So International Discipline" not having been published yet.

Kevin Dunn traces his influences further back, and believes his response to world politics was informed by the racialised context in which he grew up in the US, his interest in counter-cultural movements (he has also written about the relationship between punk and IR; (see Dunn, 2020), which eventually lead him to Africa and to the anti-apartheid struggle. His realisation of the problem of Eurocentrism in IR came later, during his PhD coursework, when he noticed that any mention of Africa was absent in his IR syllabi. Curious about whether this was a general phenomenon, he started looking at different North American IR syllabi, and came to the conclusion that the continent and scholarship about the continent was completely marginalised and ignored.

How Lily Ling's background shaped her thinking about world politics is evident in much of her work.[7] According to her, "Knowledge arises from time, place, and – significantly – feeling" (Ling, 2014: 44). In explaining worldism in her 2014 book *The Dao of World Politics*, for example, she began with an anecdote from her own life, which for her

---

[7] Lily Ling was an inspiration for many of us trying to do IR in a more global way. As someone who was constantly searching out the boundaries of scholarship - she wrote plays and fairy tales about IR - she was also deeply committed to something she called epistemic compassion. While she passed away prematurely in 2018, her work continues to inspire.

"demonstrates the wordlist nature of world politics" (Ling, 2014: 24). Recalling how, as a citizen of Taiwan and a US green card holder, she ended up at a lunch with a senior Chinese Communist Party member and foreign guests from Europe and the US whilst on a visit to Beijing in 1987 as a graduate student, she goes on to describe her experience of multiple worlds overlapping, clashing and interacting. Herself representative of and at the same time faced with a multitude of languages and cultures, political ideologies, family relations, governments, and spaces, she experienced "contradictory thoughts and feelings" (Ling, 2014: 24). Writing nearly 30 years later, she reflected, "…multiplicities in identity and subjectivity, location and position, transcend the postmodern awareness that a 'centre' or a 'master narrative' no longer holds, if it ever did" (Ling, 2014: 24).

For Siddharth Mallavarapu it was less an experience than an encounter, and not a personal one but rather one with the work of a particular author. He reminisces about coming across the books of Ashish Nandy—*The Intimate Enemy* (1988) and *Traditions, Tyrannies and Utopias* (1999)—in the university library during his undergraduate studies: "I found them so enticing and interesting, and they opened up the entire colonial question. However, what was more compelling was also the manner in which this literature probed how the self and other were reconstituted as a consequence of the encounter and how that impacted both at some deeper and more fundamental level." He adds, "of course we knew that there was a dominant core, which was imposing a certain regime of ideas of thinking, and we knew that when physical decolonisation or political decolonisation in some sense had taken place the task of intellectual decolonisation was still rather incomplete. Nandy alerted us to some of these concerns in our part of the world. However, the invitation was also to think beyond the problem of Eurocentrism. It was more broadly about imperial formations and the concentration of power in certain parts of the world along with the simultaneous exclusion or neglect of others, particularly in the Global South. What fascinated me from this slice of scholarship was how it was impacting not merely collectives but also individuals. This intersected with my exposure to subaltern studies as a distinct school of historiography that was invested in examining the role of the 'subaltern' in history both in terms of the political economy and culture. These influences were coalescing around the same time in my life. In a sense, it drew me into a distinct political ecology with a set of inflections in terms of sensibilities that have stayed with me consistently."

Pinar Bilgin recalls that when she was studying IR in Ankara at Middle East Technical University (METU), while there were IR/international politics courses that touched upon security issues, all that was covered was proliferation and deterrence. She remembers all of this "meaning really nothing to me because it was about the US-Soviet exchange…and Turkey's security only came into the discussion as part of the study of terrorism…So security courses did not seem to have any relevance beyond the low intensity conflict, terrorism dimension." Similar to Siddharth Mallavarapu encountering the work of Ashish Nandy, she came across the work of Ken Booth in an outline of a course on international security. This resulted in an interest in critical security studies (CSS, which was not called that at the time) and lead her to pursue a PhD on regional security in the Middle East with Ken Booth at the University of Wales at Aberystwyth. She believes that, had she stayed in Turkey and not gone to Aberystwyth she does not know if she would have gotten interested in any of this. For her, it was really the exposure to CCS at Aberystwyth that got her thinking differently about IR. At the same time, she identifies the discomfort she experienced when returning to Turkey from Wales: "I have been thinking about Edward Said and his notion of exile. People who feel like they don't belong but are also trying to make sense of two different worlds at the same time". Although she notes that she has always resisted studying Turkey, she admits that "coming from a non-Western setting that at the time sought to locate itself in the West but was constantly being rebuffed as it did so may have given me the context to think about these things in a way that may perhaps not have occurred to me if I was coming from a place that was considered comfortably non-Western. Or the margins of the West, central and Eastern Europe or say Germany. So positionality is important, but what you make of positionality is not unimportant. I mean I was not in exile, but I was – this is another Saidian phrase – out of place when I came back."

This sense of being out of place, experiencing a sense of puzzlement, or discomfort, or looking in from the margins (whether geographically or disciplinarily) is something all these scholars mention explicitly or implicitly. For some the interest in moving beyond IR's Eurocentrism was a result of physically relocating from one positionality (cultural, geographical, political) to another. For others it was the result of studying parts of the world that were different from the ones they themselves were based in. While this often entailed travelling to and therefore experiencing other environments this is not the only way of encountering difference. It can also happen through reading, for example. As mentioned above, Kevin Dunn's work on Africa was what initially led him to questioning the way in which IR was unable to make sense of the continent. For Arlene Tickner, questioning Western intellectual hegemony in IR began when she first engaged with IR at a university in Colombia. Pinar Bilgin was trying to make sense of how security works in the context of the Middle East, and Siddharth Mallavarapu wondered whether Indian thinkers had reflected on matters of relevance to IR. This had the effect of challenging their conceptual apparatus due to experiencing a disjuncture between what they 'knew' in one context and what they were trying to understand in another, or what they 'knew' from experience (usually in a different geocultural context) and what they were told is the 'truth' in a different geocultural setting. In other words, they were puzzled.

The way Patricia Hill talks about being an outsider from within, or being at the edges has also resonated with Arlene Tickner, who says it provides a vantage point from which you see things differently. Living in Colombia she became more attuned to the importance of everyday life – not due to the academic literature on this but because of "things that happen every day in a place like Colombia and make you sit down and pause and think how those experiences lead you to ask different questions or experience the world differently." Siddharth Mallavarapu mentions several points of estrangement. He recalls reading Kenneth Waltz for the first time, who wrote that great powers matter in world politics and we should only concern ourselves with them. This made him wonder whether countries like India and others in the Global South were of any consequence at all to the discipline that he had chosen to study, and whether he had made the right choice in choosing his field of study. He reflects on the benefits of estrangement, adding, "It's a good place to be in, and I think we should all suspend our familiar assumptions about things around us on and off. ...I think it's wonderful to be in our fields of study, where we are constantly challenged by a complex world. It's befuddling. It's a good thing that it's befuddling, because the moment we cease to think it's befuddling I think we're back to platitudes and certitudes which are not good scholarship. They're just sort of lulling us into some sort of misplaced understanding and complacency about the world."

GENEROSITY AND SERENDIPITY: A PERSONAL GENEALOGY OF EFFORTS TO ADDRESS IR'S EUROCENTRIC LIMITATIONS

Another thread that ran through all the conversations was the importance of the generosity and mentorship of specific individuals who the scholars were working closely with at a given time (for example PhD supervisors) and had a formalised or institutionalised relationship with. In addition, however, everyone mentioned random incidents that turned out to be quite significant in retrospect. These included chance meetings with people where words of encouragement were exchanged, or connections were made that would lead to contact with others who would, in turn, become significant. Often these people are not ones readily associated with efforts to address Eurocentrism in IR but who, in different ways, were supportive of it, either personally or through their institutional influence in professional organisations like the ISA.

Siddharth Mallavarapu notes that he was fortunate to have Kanti Bajpai as a doctoral advisor and mentor "Because I think he opened all of us [postgraduate students] to theorising international relations. He also alerted us to our curriculum, which was constituted then largely by Anglo-American scholars and accents. He suggested that we should go beyond this and ask questions drawing from a more immediate provenance. Do we have traditions of thinking in India or in IR theory? What does it look like? Are there people here who are also engaging these bodies of thought? If there was an aversion to theory, we needed to understand why there was an aversion to it. I'm very grateful, because that's when I felt even more spurred to immerse myself a little more in these questions and these inquiries. Another major influence was B. S. Chimni, a pioneering figure in the Third World Approaches to International Law (TWAIL) tradition. It is from him that I came to appreciate particularly how law and politics were deeply intertwined." Kevin Dunn had a similar experience with his PhD supervisor, Tim Shaw, who he says did not think in terms of disciplinary boundaries. When Kevin first approached him with his idea to do a project on IR's marginalization of the African continent, Tim was encouraging and, through his name and network, Kevin was able to secure contributors and a publisher. This resulted in the co-edited book titled *Africa's Challenge to International Relations* (Dunn & Shaw, 2001).

Arlene recalls a visit by James Rosenau to Colombia where, as one of the only English speakers, she was asked to sit next to him at a lunch.

After telling him about her PhD research into American epistemic hege-mony in IR in the Latin American context, he suggested that she widen her exploration to other world regions, and this resulted in her 2003 article "Seeing IR Differently: Notes from the Third World". She adds that the fact that the article even got published was miraculous. It had gotten a very strong rejection and a more neutral review, but one of the student editors was Colombian, and he decided to give her a revise and resubmit and it got published. She also tells of her first meeting with Ole Waever, with whom she would go on to co-edit the Routledge series on *Worlding beyond the West* (Tickner and Waever, 2009), and whose 1998 article had been a major influence on her PhD work. Having tried to contact him unsuccessfully via email, she was attending an ISA convention in 2001, where after first being rejected, she was offered a poster presenta-tion. Another student saw it and suggested that Arlene should meet their professor, who turned out to be Ole Waever. This eventually lead to a series of ISA panels and the Routledge book series. Arlene also met Steve Smith, who had been influential intellectually, at an ISA convention. He was going to be the ISA president the following year, and she suggested to him that it would be really interesting if he started looking at how IR has unfolded outside of the Global North. In response, he asked her to organise some panels. She elaborates, "And so I recruited Ole [Waever] to do a workshop and then have our first panels." To the workshop they invited people like Ann Tickner, Rob Walker, Kale Holsti, Mike Shapiro, David Blaney and Naeem Inayatullah, not all readily associated with this agenda, but open to and supportive of it.

Arlene's 2003 article was, in turn, the first one I read when, being asked to teach International Relations to first-year students at Stellen-bosch University in South Africa in the early 2000s, I started wondering about the applicability of Western theories to the African context. Around the same time I also discovered Stephanie Neumann's book and Kevin Dunn and Tim Shaw's book. My first written piece on the topic was a co-written conference paper in 2004 with my colleague at the time, Janis van der Westhuizen, on challenges to theory development in South Africa. At an ISA meeting in the mid-2000s I attended a panel organised by Arlene an Ole Waever and went to speak to Arlene afterwards. This meeting eventually resulted in an invitation to contribute to the third volume of the Routledge *Worlding beyond the West series* (see Tickner & Blaney, 2012), and many years later, co-editing *International Relations from the Global South: Worlds of Difference* with her (Tickner & Smith, 2020).

There is much to say and to criticise about the ISA, and it has received—often but not always justified—criticism over the years for its North American dominance, including the difficulty for scholars from the Global South to attend its conventions due to resource challenges and bureaucratic impediments such as visas. Nevertheless, the scholars interviewed all credit the ISA for providing a forum for like-minded scholars to meet and network. It was, of course, also the vehicle for Amitav Acharya's 2014 presidential speech, setting out his Global IR agenda. The fact that he was able to do this from the authoritative position of ISA president, and that he could allocate ISA resources, including presidential panels, to the topic, made many people who probably otherwise would not have done so, sit up and take notice.

The ISA is also where Pinar Bilgin first met Lily Ling, whose book she had reviewed. She remembers how Ole Waever and Arlene Tickner got her involved in a workshop through which she met a number of other people, including Mustapha Kamal Pasha. He in turn introduced her to Siba Grovogui and Robbie Shilliam, both of whom would be significant to her thinking. She says that being asked to contribute to the Routledge book series also triggered more questions about what security from an Arab perspective looks like, "because there was this notion of Arab national security that I encountered, and I did not really know how to make sense of it. I was already aware that this was a different way of thinking about security, but I was not able to theorise about it." This changed when Ole Waever invited her to be part of the geocultural epistemologies group in 2004, in response to which she wrote a paper on the study of security in Turkey, "a country that has very different security concerns, yet the study is shaped entirely by concepts that are learned by the author depending on wherever they did their PhD apparently". She says she was not able to make sense of this, and writing that chapter was her first entry into these discussions. Arlene suggested that she bring in a comparative perspective and she ended up juxtaposing the study of Turkey and the study of security in the Arab world, finding that "in one country you have repetition of concepts without actually making proper use of them for insights, and in the other one you have something entirely different". She tried to figure out what to make of this, which became the chapter in *Thinking International Relations Differently* (Tickner & Blaney, 2012). So, she explains, "while it looks the same, it is actually different, but that difference takes different forms in different parts of the world." Underlining the significance of chance encounters, she mentions how she was working on these questions whilst in Washington DC for a sabbatical in 2007/8, where she ran into Peter Mandaville, who she knew from her PhD days. In the meantime, he, together with Stephen Chan and Roland Bleiker, had brought out the book *The Zen of International Relations* (2001). She remembers, "So I ran into him and told him what I was doing, and he said: read Itty Abraham. This is happening in a Whole Foods shop - I think it was the vegetable section. So, I went back, found the Itty Abraham book [Abraham, 1998]—a historical study of India's approach to nuclear energy and then the nuclear bomb—and read it. This lead to an article which she had initially formulated for a roundtable which Mustapha Kamal Pasha had organised for the ISA. It was about the study of security in Turkey, but this time she brought in the India dimension, and the China dimension because she had read Lily Ling's work by then. That is how she formulated the idea of 'differently different' (Bilgin, 2008), almost the same but not quite – she had read Homi Bhabha through Lily's work. She adds, "So, a number of things were coming together through my now intensive reading of postcolonial approaches to international relations."

It was at an ISA-ABRI meeting in Rio in 2009 that I presented a paper in which I cited Pinar's article. Arlene Tickner was sitting in the front row and as I mentioned it she shouted out "She's here!", pointing to Pinar who was sitting a few rows back. This led to the first meeting between Pinar and I which, 15 years later, resulted in the co-authorship of this book. At the next ISA meeting in San Diego a few of us (including Arlene Tickner, Pinar Bilgin, Lily Ling, Nizar Messari, and João Pontes Nogueira) met to discuss the need for a textbook, which after many twists and turns resulted in *International Relations from the Global South: Worlds of Difference* (Tickner & Smith, 2021).

Around the same time, I travelled to India for the first time at the end of 2009, and thought I would use the opportunity to find out who in India was doing work on non-Western IR. Through somewhat random Internet searches involving trawling through Indian university websites, I happened upon Kanti Bajpai and Siddharth Mallavarapu at Jawaharlal Nehru University (JNU), who generously responded to my emails. Kanti Bajpai, who was at the time taking a break from academia and was the headmaster at the prestigious Doon School in Deradun, kindly offered to meet me in Delhi in what for me was a most insightful conversation. Together with his then PhD student Siddharth Mallavarapu, he had co-edited two volumes on IR theory and India (Bajpai and Mallavarapu, 2005 and 2005b) which were not available outside of India at the time, but which I then managed to acquire at a bookshop near the JNU campus, with the help of Siddharth Mallavarapu, who I met a few weeks later. Siddharth would, in turn, some years later, introduce me to his then PhD student Vineet Thakur, with whom I co-edited a special issue on the multiple births of IR in 2021 (Thakur & Smith, 2021). The point of this personal reflection is to underline the importance of personal connections and of chance encounters in the development of one's work and interests. As IR students and researchers we sometimes experience a lot of pressure in choosing the 'right' research topic or approach, or networking with the 'right' people. In reality, research topics and collaborations often choose us – through things we read, things we see, people we speak to, things that excite or frustrate us.

WHERE TO FROM HERE?

Kevin Dunn notes how his thinking about how to go about addressing Eurocentrism has changed over time. "I used to think we have to ignore all of the mainstream theories. But that's not where I am now. I think that further marginalises conversations with people who might dismiss us anyway. We have to understand our master's tools but not be enslaved by them (but on another day I might say that by using the master's tools we'll always be enslaved)." Following the line of thinking that ideas are the result of interconnections, we should perhaps first ask whether the tools are in fact the master's tools.[8] He adds, "My position has probably changed over time but there is still a huge part of me that is still a good Gramscian who understands hegemony and is always trying to think about the ways in which to engage, and about counter-hegemonic practices. I don't think there is *a* way. I think one assaults hegemony in as many ways as one can...and I think that within IR...I wouldn't want to close off any possibilities of counter-hegemonic practices." Siddharth Mallavarapu shares this view, contending, "I think there's no one size fits

---

[8] See the discussion in Chapter 3 on this point.

all here, really. And I believe different scholars should take a jab at it with what they're most comfortable with."

The scholars I engaged with share a concern with starting with the empirical and not the abstract, the theoretical. Kevin suggests that students interested in pursuing research in this area ask themselves where they are seeing Eurocentrism. He notes that they are experiencing the world of a globalised IR in different ways to the way in which it was experienced 20 years ago, so they need to start with articulating where *they* see the problem. "Where are the voices not being heard and how can we address that? That can then lead them to research areas/questions/methods," he suggests. He is also still a fan of area studies as a way into IR, and emphasises how conversations with area studies colleagues working on other regions can be particularly enriching.

Arlene Tickner similarly calls on researchers to tap into their epistemic discomfort. In other words, what makes them uncomfortable in the world, or about the world, or makes them angry or upset or passionate. She adds, "And then you kind of have to push on those discomforts and think about questions". In terms of her own work, she has moved from what might be regarded as a geocultural approach to more recent reflections on relationality. She notes, "I get bored of things really easily, just to be clear. So that's kind of why I changed my questions. And I'm not well schooled. I studied mathematics in college, then did a PhD in IR under tremendously difficult circumstances, with two babies. So I'm not well read, I'm not well trained. And I think that just kind of means that I don't really get hung up on existing literature. I kind of just go with what I find that seems interesting. It's sometimes quite random, if you want." Her work is driven both by scholars who write interesting things that she comes across, but also just looking at the world and getting angry or interested about stuff. She admits that she is "very empirical, in kind of a visceral sense." In terms of the way forward and reflecting on the recent turn to relationality, she notes, "I'm all for that reflection, but I just think that the debates have become so far removed from reality that I just reached a point where I started feeling it was senseless, and I decided if I was going to continue working on this, at least to have some contact on the ground with groups about whose cosmovisions I was talking about." Elaborating on this point, she explains that what resonates most with her today is "the importance of striking up genuine and meaningful dialogues or conversations with actors, especially vulnerable social actors on the grounds, with an eye to re-crafting the concepts and know-how with which we make sense of the world and with which we can then construct more meaningful policies to deal with all the problems". One thing she has found tremendously useful is thinking from below, including making public policy through participatory processes. She notes how in her current position as the Colombian deputy permanent representative to the UN, she is seeing in practice how important that is.

Kevin Dunn cautions against adopting exclusionary or self-marginalising labels such as globalising or decolonising IR and notes that he is more interested in the conversations and the solutions rather than worrying about whichever camp he would position himself in. At the same time, he recognises that "for some, identifying with a group is not only intellectual, it's also a form of self-care and nurturing one's identity." On focusing on difference, he cautions: "I try not to inhabit the exceptionalism argument. Every place, every continent, case study has its unique aspects but there are elements of similarity. The African continent and African experiences are hugely diverse – there is no 'African experience' in IR. It's not that they are so exceptionally different to other places, it's that they are different enough and that in their difference they highlight the ways in which the established theories are mistaken or they're making really limited assumptions. One can think in terms of a metaphor of a cloth or fabric[9]: in the middle of the fabric where it's tightly woven you can't actually see much, while at the edge of the margins you can start pulling it apart. In terms of a core-periphery analysis, when you're at the periphery you can see the ways in which the system is structured, and you lose that perspective if you are only focusing on experiences at the core."

As general advice to students and researchers, Siddharth Mallavarapu suggests to read widely. He cites the political scientist and anthropologist James Scott,[10] who said that at least one third of what you read should be outside your discipline. He also emphasises the importance of widening one's horizons by adopting a comparative frame, which in turn gives you a different perspective of your own country, and praises the benefits accrued from displacement. While geographical displacement

---

[9] Also see Tickner and Querejazu (2021) in which they use weaving as a metaphor for entanglement and interconnection.

[10] See the interview with Scott in Munck and Snyder (2007).

is one strategy, another form of displacement can be to travel through books and ideas and frames and canvases. As he notes, these days "you can do it anywhere you are located in the world today, thanks in part to Professor Google and the others." Along these lines, and drawing inspiration from Rebecca Solnit (2005) he encourages all of us to get lost, in the best sense of the term.

CONCLUSION

Many overviews of attempts to address Eurocentrism in IR start with the 'globalising turn'—and specifically with Amitav Acharya's 2014 article. While he may have coined the term "Global IR" he was of course building on a foundation of work that goes back much further. The turn has garnered much momentum in recent years, due to related societal developments that have facilitated an interest in questions of decolonisation (although this too is an over-used buzzword), addressing and recognising silences in the field, including the role of race and empire. While it is important for the development of knowledge that scholars build on and challenge existing ideas, doing so selectively and not engaging with a longer history of scholarship runs the risk of reinventing the wheel, or building straw men who are then criticised in a self-congratulatory manner. Relatedly, when we look back we can be critical about paths or positions not taken, but we also need to be heedful of what was possible within the constraints of the day. Ideas that would have been dismissed out of hand not so long ago are now increasingly tolerated – if not entirely accepted. As outlined in Chapter 2, over the course of decades, a handful of people laid the foundations for what became possible later.

BIBLIOGRAPHY

Abraham, I. (1998). *The Making of the Indian Atomic Bomb: Science, Secrecy and the Postcolonial State*. Zed Books.

Acharya, A. (2014). Global International Relations (IR) and Regional Worlds: A New Agenda for International Studies. *International Studies Quarterly, 58*(4), 647–659.

Alden, C. and Aran, A. (2012). *Foreign Policy Analysis: New Approaches*. Routledge.

Ayoob, M.H. (2002). Inequality and Theorizing in International Relations: The Case for Subaltern Realism. *International Studies Review, 4*, 27-48.

Bajpai, K. P., & Mallavarapu, S. (Eds.). (2005a). *International Relations in India: Bringing Theory Back Home.* Orient Longman.

Bajpai, K. P., & Mallavarapu, S. (Eds.). (2005b). *International Relations in India: Theorizing the Region and Nation.* Orient Longman.

Bilgin, P. (2008). Thinking Past 'Western' IR? *Third World Quarterly, 29*(1), 5-23.

Bilgin, P. (2016a). Edward Said's 'contrapuntal Reading' as a Method, an Ethos and a Metaphor for Global IR. *International Studies Review, 18*(1), 134–146.

Bilgin, P. (2016b). Do IR Scholars Engage with the Same World? In K. Booth & T. Erskine (Eds.), *International Relations Theory Today* (2nd. ed.). Polity.

Bilgin, P. (2016c). *The International in Security, Security in the International.* Routledge.

Çalkivik, A. (2020). Foreign Policy. In A.B. Tickner & K. Smith (Eds.). (2020). *International Relations from the Global South: Worlds of Difference (1st ed.).* Routledge.

Callahan, W.A. (2008). Chinese Visions of World Order: Post-hegemonic or a New Hegemony?, *International Studies Review, 10*(4), 749–761.

Campbell, D. (1998). *Writing Security: United States Foreign Policy and the Politics of Identity.* University of Minnesota.

Chan, S., Mandaville, P., and Bleiker, R. (2001). *The Zen of International Relations: IR Theory from East to West.* Palgrave Macmillan.

Chen, C. C., & Shimizu, K. (2019). International relations from the margins: the Westphalian meta-narratives and counter-narratives in Okinawa–Taiwan relations. *Cambridge Review of International Affairs, 32*(4), 521–540.

Chimni, B. S., & Mallavarapu, S. (Eds.). (2012) *International Relations: Perspectives for the Global South.* Pearson.

Dunn, K. (2003). *Imagining the Congo: The International Relations of Identity.* Palgrave Macmillan.

Dunn, K. (2020). *Global Punk: Resistance and Rebellion in Everyday Life.* Bloomsbury Academic.

Dunn, K., & Englebert, P. (2020). *Inside African Politics: 2nd Edition.* Lynne Rienner Press.

Escudé, C. (1998)."An Introduction to Peripheral Realism". In S.G. Neuman (Ed.). *International Relations Theory and the Third World.* (pp.55-75). St. Martin's Press.

Hansen, L. (2006). *Security as Practice: Discourse Analysis and the Bosnian War.* Francis & Taylor.

Hoffman, S. (1977). An American Social Science: International Relations. *Daedalus, 106*(3), 41–60.

Herborth, B. (2015). Do We Need 195 Theories of Foreign Policy? In G. Hellman and K.E. Jorgensen (Eds.). *Theorizing Foreign Policy in a Globalized World.* (pp.101-125), Palgrave Macmillan.

Jordaan, E. (2003). The concept of a middle power in international relations: distinguishing between emerging and traditional middle powers. *Politikon*, *30*(1), 165–181.

Kavalski, E. (2016). Review: Relationality and Its Chinese Characteristics, *The China Quarterly*, 226 (June), 551–559.

Laffey, M. & Weldes, J. (2008). Decolonizing the Cuban Missile Crisis, *International Studies Quarterly*, *52*(3), 555–577.

Ling, L. H. M. (2014). *The Dao of World Politics: Towards a Post-Westphalian, Worldist International Relations*. Routledge.

Messari, N. (2001). Identity and Foreign Policy – The Case of Islam in US Foreign Policy. In V. Kubalkova (Ed.). *Foreign Policy in a Constructed World* (pp.227–248). ME Sharpe.

Munck, G. L., and Snyder, R. (2007). Interview with James C. Scott: Peasants, Power, and the Art of Resistance. In G. L. Munck & R. Snyder (Eds.), *Passion, Craft and Method in Comparative Politics* (pp. 351–391). *Passion, Craft and Method in Comparative Politics*. Johns Hopkins University Press.

Nandy, A. (1988). *The Intimate Enemy: Loss and Recovery of Self Under Colonialism*. Oxford University Press.

Nandy, A. (1999). *Traditions, Tyrannies, and Utopias: Essays in the Politics Of Awareness*. Oxford University Press.

Neuman, S. G. (1998). International Relations Theory and the Third World: An Oxymoron? In S. G. Neuman (Ed.), *International Relations Theory and the Third World* (pp. 1–29). Macmillan.

Qin, Y. (2020). Diplomacy as Relational Practice. *The Hague Journal of Diplomacy*, *15*(1–2), 165–173.

Schoeman, M. (2000). South Africa as an emerging middle power. *African Security Review*, *9*(3), 47–58.

Shih, C-Y. & Huang, C-C. (2015). China's Quest for Grand Strategy: Power, National Interest, or Relational Security?, *The Chinese Journal of International Politics*, *8*(1), 1–26.

Shih, C.-Y. (2016). Affirmative Balance of the Singapore–Taiwan Relationship: A Bilateral Perspective on the Relational Turn in International Relations. *International Studies Review*, *18*(4), 681–701.

Smith, S., Hadfield, A., & Dunne, T. (Eds.) (2016). *Foreign Policy: Theories, Actors, Cases* (3rd ed.). Oxford University Press.

Solnit, R. (2005). *A Field Guide to Getting Lost*. Viking.

Thakur, V., & Smith, K. (2021). Introduction to the Special Issue: The Multiple Births of International Relations. *Review of International Studies*, *47*(5), 571–579.

Tickner, A. (2003). Seeing IR Differently: Notes from the Third World. *Millennium-Journal of International Studies*, *32*(2), 295–324.

Tickner, A. B., & Blaney, D. (Eds.). (2012). *Thinking International Relations Differently* (Vol. 2). Routledge.

Tickner, A. B., & Smith, K. (2020). *International Relations from the Global South: Worlds of Difference*. Routledge.

Tickner, A. B., & Waever, O. (Eds.). (2009). *International Relations Scholarship Around the World*. Routledge.

Waever, O. (1998). The Sociology of a Not So International Discipline: American and European Developments in International Relations. *International Organization, 52*(4), 687–727.

Zhao, T. (2009). A political world. *Diogenes, 56*(5), 5-18.

Zhao, T. (2021). *All under heaven: The tianxia system for a possible world order*. University of California Press.

INDEX

© The Editor(s) (if applicable) and The Author(s), under exclusive license to Springer Nature Switzerland AG 2024
P. Bilgin and K. Smith, *Thinking Globally About World Politics: Beyond Global IR*, https://doi.org/10.1007/978-3-031-56572-4

155

GPSR Compliance

The European Union's (EU) General Product Safety Regulation (GPSR) is a set of rules that requires consumer products to be safe and our obligations to ensure this.

If you have any concerns about our products, you can contact us on ProductSafety@springernature.com

In case Publisher is established outside the EU, the EU authorized representative is:

Springer Nature Customer Service Center GmbH
Europaplatz 3
69115 Heidelberg, Germany

The manufacturer's authorised representative in the EU is Springer
Nature Customer Service Centre GmbH, Europaplatz 3, 69115 Heidelberg,
Germany. If you have any concerns regarding our products, please
contact ProductSafety@springernature.com

Printed and bound by CPI Group (UK) Ltd, Croydon, CR0 4YY

24/04/2026

02096315-0014